# EXPLORING THE WORLD OF MAMMALS

## VOLUME 3

Gaz–Koa

**CHELSEA HOUSE**
PUBLISHERS
An imprint of Infobase Publishing

Copyright © 2008 The Brown Reference Group plc

**Chelsea House**
An imprint of Infobase Publishing
132 West 31st Street
New York, NY 10001

**Library of Congress Cataloging-in-Publication Data**

Exploring the world of mammals / [edited by Nancy Simmons, Richard Beatty, Amy-Jane Beer]. -- 1st ed.
    p. cm.
  Includes index.
  ISBN-13: 978-0-7910-9651-2
  ISBN-10: 0-7910-9651-3
  1.  Mammals--Juvenile literature.  I. Simmons, Nancy B. II. Beatty, Richard. III. Beer, Amy-Jane. IV. Title.

  QL706.2.E97 2008
  599--dc22

2007028223

Printed and bound in China

**For The Brown Reference Group plc**
Project Editor: Lesley Ellis
Designer: Graham Curd
Picture Researcher: Laila Torsun
Indexer: Kay Ollerenshaw
Cartographer: Darren Awuah
Design Manager: Sarah Williams
Managing Editor: Bridget Giles
Editorial Director: Lindsey Lowe

**Consultant Editor**
Professor Nancy Simmons
Chair, Division of Vertebrate Zoology,
Curator-in-Charge at the Department of Mammology,
American Museum of Natural History, New York

**Authors**
Richard Beatty; Amy-Jane Beer; Jen Green; Barbara Taylor

# CONTENTS

# INTRODUCING MAMMALS

Asked to describe a mammal, most people might say, quite correctly, a warm, furry animal that feeds its young on milk. There are around 5,000 different species of mammals, all of which have hair or fur, a constant internal body temperature (are "warm-blooded"), and feed their offspring on milk. The milk is usually produced from special skin organs called mammary glands. However, not all mammals look alike. Bats, bears, whales, wallabies, hedgehogs, and hippopotamuses—each of these extremely diverse animals is a mammal. Humans are mammals, too, and are grouped with chimpanzees, gorillas, and orangutans.

Between them, mammals have adapted their body shapes and behaviors to live practically all over the world and are therefore among the most successful animals on Earth. Some mammals can fly, some can swim, while others burrow below ground, run or jump across the surface, or climb trees. Some mammals, such as polar bears and dolphins, are carnivores and eat only meat; others, such as giraffes and pronghorn, are herbivores, or plant eaters. Many other species of mammals are omnivores that eat both plants and animals. Omnivores include raccoons and badgers.

The three main groups of mammals are the egg-laying monotremes (platypus and echidnas); marsupials, such as koalas, kangaroos, and opossums, which give birth to highly undeveloped offspring and raise them in pouches; and placentals, the females of which nuture their babies inside their body in the uterus before giving birth to well-developed young.

## Exploring the World of Mammals

From aardvarks to wombats, these six volumes of *Exploring the World of Mammals* provide more than one hundred articles that describe in detail particular species and groups of mammals. Most are general articles about individual mammal species, such as colobus monkeys, hippopotamuses, or tapirs. Other articles are more specific, providing an overview of an entire order (large group) of mammals, such as bats or carnivores, or a family of mammals, such as bears or cats. These specific articles are shown in bold type on the table of contents in each volume.

Each volume has a number of useful features, including: a mammalian family tree, which shows how mammals fit into the animal kingdom, how they are related to one another, and provides cross references to articles in this encyclopedia; a glossary of terms used throughout the set; a section entitled Further resources, which includes further reading and Internet resources; and a volume-specific index. Volume 6 contains a complete set index.

Every article has a Fact File box, which summarizes a mammal's family and order, explains how many species exist, and shows a detailed map of where the mammal lives. In addition, there are facts about the mammal's habitat, size, coat, diet, breeding, life span, and status according to the World Conservation Union (IUCN; see opposite). Other items include boxes that provide more in-depth information about specific details and a Did You Know? feature that presents interesting facts about specific mammals. Throughout, there are large, colorful photographs and illustrations that increase the reader's enjoyment and enhance an understanding of the world of mammals.

## Carnivore, herbivore, insect eater, or omnivore?

**A**bove the Fact File in each general article is a colored tag and a small illustration that highlights whether a particular mammal is a carnivore (meat eater), an insect eater, a herbivore (plant eater), or an omnivore (one that eats both plants and animals). As a general description here, *carnivore* describes any mammal that eats animal food, rather than more specifically a member of the order (large group) of mammals called Carnivora. Aardvarks and anteaters are listed as insect eaters because they eat ants and termites, but they are also carnivores because they eat animal food. The category chosen for each article covers the majority of members of the group of mammals being described and the bulk of the animal's diet. For example, baboons and macaques are described as omnivores because most species eat both plant and animal food. However, the gelada baboon eats only grass, which makes it a herbivore. Similarly, gorillas are listed as herbivores (plant eaters) because they eat mostly leaves, fruit, shoots, and bark, although they also eat a few termites and caterpillars.

**CARNIVORES**

**HERBIVORES**

**INSECT EATERS**

**OMNIVORES**

## World Conservation Union (IUCN)

The World Conservation Union (IUCN) is the world's largest and most important conservation network. Its mission is to help protect all living organisms and natural resources by highlighting those threatened with extinction and therefore promote their conservation.

An organism may be placed in one of the following categories in the *IUCN Red List of Threatened Species*:

**Extinct**—there is no reasonable doubt that the last individual has died

**Extinct in the wild**—an organism survives only in captivity, in cultivation, or as a population well outside its past range

**Critically endangered**—facing an extremely high risk of extinction in the wild

**Endangered**—facing a very high risk of extinction in the wild

**Vulnerable**—facing a high risk of extinction in the wild

**Near threatened**—likely to qualify for a threatened category in the near future

**Least concern**—is not threatened

**Data deficient**—inadequate information exists to make an assessment

The status of each mammal or group of mammals according to the IUCN is highlighted at the foot of the Fact File in every article.

## Classifying mammals

Scientists group together, or classify, animals that have a common ancestor and therefore share similar physical features and genes (sections of DNA, or deoxyribonucleic acid). That common ancestor might have lived millions of years ago. The family tree shown overleaf reveals the relationships among mammals. All mammals belong to the class Mammalia, which is divided into several large groups called orders that contain more closely related mammals. In turn, each order of mammals is divided into smaller groups called families, which contain even more closely related mammals. For example, the order Cetacea includes all whales and dolphins. Within this order are several families, including Delphinidae, which covers dolphins. Delphinidae is further divided into seventeen smaller groups called genera (singular genus), which contain several individual species, or types, of dolphins. The species is the smallest category of biological classification. Animals belonging to the same species can breed together successfully to produce fertile offspring.

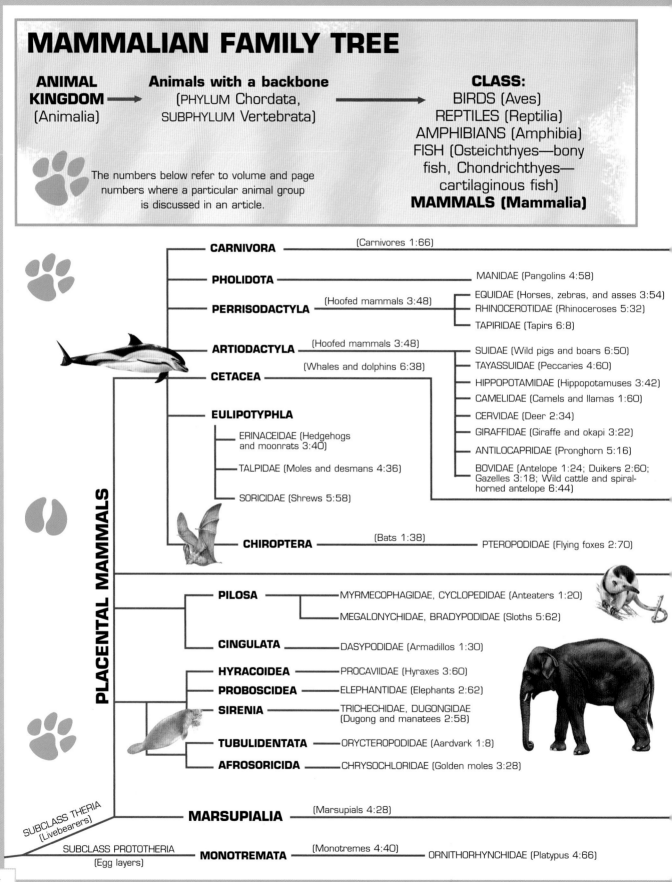

# MAMMALIAN FAMILY TREE

**ANIMAL KINGDOM** (Animalia) →

**Animals with a backbone** (PHYLUM Chordata, SUBPHYLUM Vertebrata) →

**CLASS:**
BIRDS (Aves)
REPTILES (Reptilia)
AMPHIBIANS (Amphibia)
FISH (Osteichthyes—bony fish, Chondrichthyes—cartilaginous fish)
**MAMMALS (Mammalia)**

The numbers below refer to volume and page numbers where a particular animal group is discussed in an article.

**PLACENTAL MAMMALS**

**CARNIVORA** — (Carnivores 1:66)

**PHOLIDOTA** — MANIDAE (Pangolins 4:58)

**PERRISODACTYLA** — (Hoofed mammals 3:48)
- EQUIDAE (Horses, zebras, and asses 3:54)
- RHINOCEROTIDAE (Rhinoceroses 5:32)
- TAPIRIDAE (Tapirs 6:8)

**ARTIODACTYLA** — (Hoofed mammals 3:48)
- SUIDAE (Wild pigs and boars 6:50)
- TAYASSUIDAE (Peccaries 4:60)
- HIPPOPOTAMIDAE (Hippopotamuses 3:42)
- CAMELIDAE (Camels and llamas 1:60)
- CERVIDAE (Deer 2:34)
- GIRAFFIDAE (Giraffe and okapi 3:22)
- ANTILOCAPRIDAE (Pronghorn 5:16)
- BOVIDAE (Antelope 1:24; Duikers 2:60; Gazelles 3:18; Wild cattle and spiral-horned antelope 6:44)

**CETACEA** — (Whales and dolphins 6:38)

**EULIPOTYPHLA**
- ERINACEIDAE (Hedgehogs and moonrats 3:40)
- TALPIDAE (Moles and desmans 4:36)
- SORICIDAE (Shrews 5:58)

**CHIROPTERA** — (Bats 1:38) — PTEROPODIDAE (Flying foxes 2:70)

**PILOSA**
- MYRMECOPHAGIDAE, CYCLOPEDIDAE (Anteaters 1:20)
- MEGALONYCHIDAE, BRADYPODIDAE (Sloths 5:62)

**CINGULATA** — DASYPODIDAE (Armadillos 1:30)

**HYRACOIDEA** — PROCAVIIDAE (Hyraxes 3:60)

**PROBOSCIDEA** — ELEPHANTIDAE (Elephants 2:62)

**SIRENIA** — TRICHECHIDAE, DUGONGIDAE (Dugong and manatees 2:58)

**TUBULIDENTATA** — ORYCTEROPODIDAE (Aardvark 1:8)

**AFROSORICIDA** — CHRYSOCHLORIDAE (Golden moles 3:28)

SUBCLASS THERIA (Livebearers)

**MARSUPIALIA** — (Marsupials 4:28)

SUBCLASS PROTOTHERIA (Egg layers)

**MONOTREMATA** — (Monotremes 4:40) — ORNITHORHYNCHIDAE (Platypus 4:66)

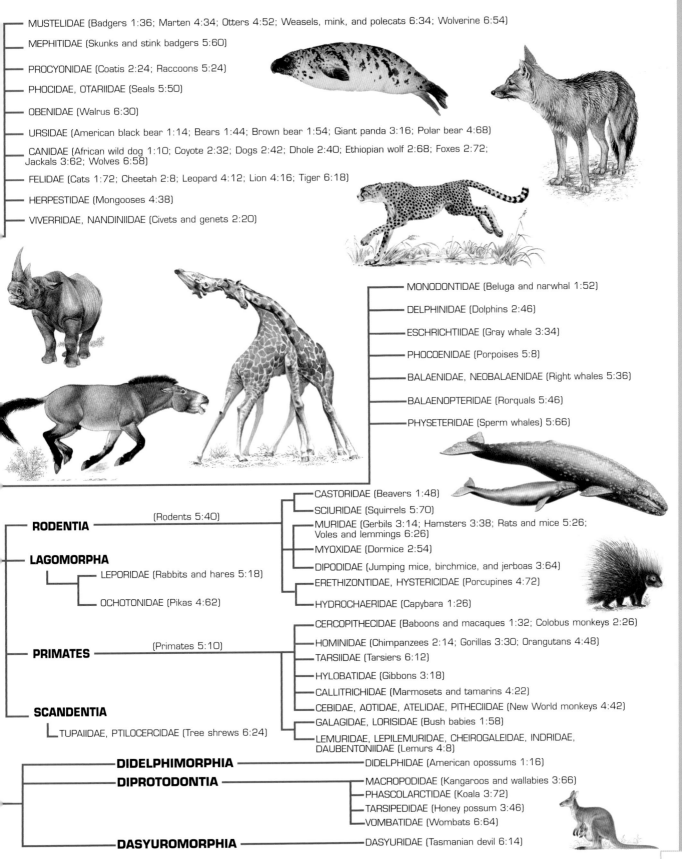

MUSTELIDAE (Badgers 1:36; Marten 4:34; Otters 4:52; Weasels, mink, and polecats 6:34; Wolverine 6:54)

MEPHITIDAE (Skunks and stink badgers 5:60)

PROCYONIDAE (Coatis 2:24; Raccoons 5:24)

PHOCIDAE, OTARIIDAE (Seals 5:50)

OBENIDAE (Walrus 6:30)

URSIDAE (American black bear 1:14; Bears 1:44; Brown bear 1:54; Giant panda 3:16; Polar bear 4:68)

CANIDAE (African wild dog 1:10; Coyote 2:32; Dogs 2:42; Dhole 2:40; Ethiopian wolf 2:68; Foxes 2:72; Jackals 3:62; Wolves 6:58)

FELIDAE (Cats 1:72; Cheetah 2:8; Leopard 4:12; Lion 4:16; Tiger 6:18)

HERPESTIDAE (Mongooses 4:38)

VIVERRIDAE, NANDINIIDAE (Civets and genets 2:20)

MONODONTIDAE (Beluga and narwhal 1:52)

DELPHINIDAE (Dolphins 2:46)

ESCHRICHTIIDAE (Gray whale 3:34)

PHOCOENIDAE (Porpoises 5:8)

BALAENIDAE, NEOBALAENIDAE (Right whales 5:36)

BALAENOPTERIDAE (Rorquals 5:46)

PHYSETERIDAE (Sperm whales) 5:66)

CASTORIDAE (Beavers 1:48)

SCIURIDAE (Squirrels 5:70)

MURIDAE (Gerbils 3:14; Hamsters 3:38; Rats and mice 5:26; Voles and lemmings 6:26)

MYOXIDAE (Dormice 2:54)

DIPODIDAE (Jumping mice, birchmice, and jerboas 3:64)

ERETHIZONTIDAE, HYSTERICIDAE (Porcupines 4:72)

HYDROCHAERIDAE (Capybara 1:26)

**RODENTIA** — (Rodents 5:40)

**LAGOMORPHA**

LEPORIDAE (Rabbits and hares 5:18)

OCHOTONIDAE (Pikas 4:62)

CERCOPITHECIDAE (Baboons and macaques 1:32; Colobus monkeys 2:26)

HOMINIDAE (Chimpanzees 2:14; Gorillas 3:30; Orangutans 4:48)

TARSIIDAE (Tarsiers 6:12)

**PRIMATES** — (Primates 5:10)

HYLOBATIDAE (Gibbons 3:18)

CALLITRICHIDAE (Marmosets and tamarins 4:22)

CEBIDAE, AOTIDAE, ATELIDAE, PITHECIIDAE (New World monkeys 4:42)

GALAGIDAE, LORISIDAE (Bush babies 1:58)

**SCANDENTIA**

TUPAIIDAE, PTILOCERCIDAE (Tree shrews 6:24)

LEMURIDAE, LEPILEMURIDAE, CHEIROGALEIDAE, INDRIDAE, DAUBENTONIIDAE (Lemurs 4:8)

**DIDELPHIMORPHIA** — DIDELPHIDAE (American opossums 1:16)

**DIPROTODONTIA** — MACROPODIDAE (Kangaroos and wallabies 3:66)

PHASCOLARCTIDAE (Koala 3:72)

TARSIPEDIDAE (Honey possum 3:46)

VOMBATIDAE (Wombats 6:64)

**DASYUROMORPHIA** — DASYURIDAE (Tasmanian devil 6:14)

7

# GAZELLES

Gazelles are among nature's supreme athletes. They have speed, agility, and grace as well as sharp senses always alert to danger. All of these features are essential to help them stay one step ahead of their many predators.

**G**azelles are the most graceful members of the cattle family. They are slender animals, with long, slim legs, a long neck, and an elegant, narrow face. Gazelles live in grasslands and on dry plains, where there is very little shelter and few places to hide from predators. Most of the distinctive features of gazelles help them survive in these open spaces.

Most gazelle species live in large groups called herds. Some herds contain hundreds or even thousands of gazelles. With many pairs of eyes and ears always checking for danger, it is extremely difficult for even the stealthiest predator to sneak up. Gazelles have large eyes that are set on the sides of the head and bulge out slightly. So, a gazelle can see to either side without having to turn its head. Gazelles have long eyelashes, which shade the eyes from the bright sun and collect dust that drifts down from the air. Gazelles also have large ears, which can turn to the sides and even backward. The ears are furry on the backs and on the insides to protect them from sunburn and from dust.

## Speedy Runners

Gazelles are famous for their speed and nimbleness. Most gazelles can run fast and, if they are being chased, they can change direction in an instant. By dodging from side to side, gazelles can even escape the fastest hunter of all, the cheetah, which can reach top speed only by running in a straight line.

*A springbok displays its characteristically curved horns. These graceful gazelles live in the dry, open plains of southern Africa, as far north as Angola.*

## Fact File

**GAZELLES**

**Family:** Bovidae; subfamily Antilopinae (more than 30 species)

**Order:** Artiodactyla

**Where do they live?** Africa, the Middle East, and parts of southern and central Asia

Equator

**Habitat:** Forests, savanna and steppe grasslands, deserts, and rocky landscapes

**Size:** Head–body length 18–68 inches (45–172 cm); weight 3.3–188 pounds (1.5–85 kg); females larger than males

**Coat:** Short and neat; coarse or silky; color and markings vary with species; most offer some camouflage

**Diet:** Grass, herbs, leaves, shoots, buds, and fruit of various shrubs and trees

**Breeding:** 140–225 days' gestation; single offspring; saiga often has twins

**Life span:** 10–18 years, depending on species and living conditions

**Status:** Around one-quarter of all gazelle species are vulnerable or endangered, some critically so

*A small herd of Thomson's gazelles gathers to eat and drink at a water hole, remaining alert for predators.*

## DID YOU KNOW?

🐾 The royal antelope is the smallest member of the gazelle group—about the size and weight of a house cat!

🐾 Springbok were once so common that their migrating herds stretched for miles!

🐾 The saiga is the only gazelle that regularly has twins.

## Locking Horns

The horns of most gazelles are not straight or smooth. Usually they are ringed with ridges and curve from the base to the tips to form an "S" shape, a "C" shape, or a spiral.

Along with their horizontal ridges, these horn shapes allow rival gazelles to lock horns firmly in combat. Male gazelles lock horns to test each other's

## KEEP ENEMIES CLOSE

Thomson's gazelles (above) have a surprising way of dealing with predators —they follow them. If a member of a herd of Thomson's gazelles spots a lion, hyena, or wild dog, it sounds the alarm, and the whole group turns to face the danger and begins to walk toward the predator. The gazelles are careful never go close enough to be in real danger. With the element of surprise lost, the predator has to slink away.

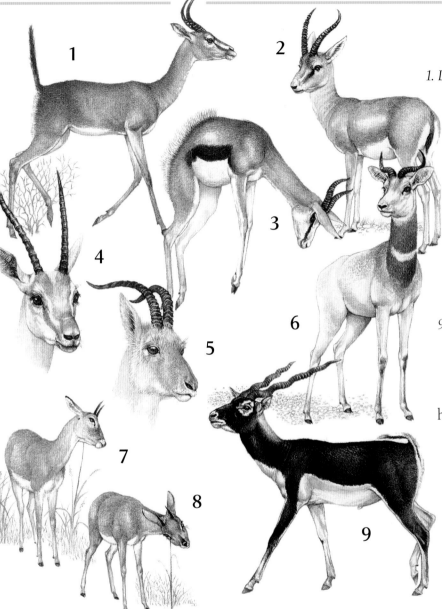

1. Dibatag in alarmed posture.
2. Goitered gazelle
3. Springbok, pronking
4. Tibetan gazelle
5. Slender-horned gazelle
6. Dama gazelle, the largest gazelle
7. Oribi, marking a stem with its ear gland
8. Steenbok, scent marking with its facial gland
9. Blackbuck, in territorial display pose

horns, and they use them to challenge each other for food and territory.

**Scent Marking**

Scent is important to most gazelles. These animals have an excellent sense of smell, and most gazelles produce scent from glands in the face (orbital glands) and the feet (pedal glands). Gazelles also release scent into their droppings. Male gazelles use dung piles to mark their territory and add fresh droppings regularly. Any intruder will know immediately that the area is already occupied.

strength without there being a serious risk of them getting hurt. It soon becomes clear which gazelle is the strongest, and the loser backs off without suffering anything worse than hurt pride. In most species, both male and female gazelles have

## A SPRING IN THEIR STEP

The springbok is named for its habit of leaping high into the air, usually with all four legs locked straight. Stretchy leg muscles and tendons absorb the energy of each bounce with each landing and catapault the animal up into the air again. Lots of other gazelles use the same trick, which is called pronking or stotting. Pronking is a way of raising the alarm, while at the same time allowing the gazelle to get a good look around. This activity probably also confuses a predator because it can be difficult to predict which way the gazelle will leap next.

## Grazers and Browsers

Gazelles are herbivores, or plant eaters. Species such as springboks and Thomson's gazelles graze on fresh grass, and they are able to smell rain from many miles away. They travel long distances to find good, fresh pasture. Other species eat the leaves and shoots of trees and shrubs. This way of eating is called browsing.

The gerenuk is a long-legged, long-necked species. It has a neat trick to help it reach higher branches than any other gazelle species–it can stand and walk on its hind legs.

## Dwarf Antelope and Dik-diks

There are eighteen species of gazelles, living in Africa and Asia. Dwarf antelope and dik-dik, close relatives of gazelles, are small and usually live in forests or more wooded habitats only in Africa. Often, they live alone or in pairs rather than in large herds. Only dwarf antelope males usually have horns. Some species, such as oribis, klipspringers, and steenboks, have short, straight, and smooth horns. These horns are stabbing weapons. These animals are more aggressive than gazelles and can kill each other when they fight.

## The Hardy Saiga

The last member of the gazelle group, the saiga, looks like the odd one out. Its legs are short and its body is stout and clumsy looking. Instead of a small, fine-featured face, it has a large head with a Roman nose and a short, floppy trunk. Saigas live on the open steppe and stony deserts of central Asia and Mongolia. Life is tough here, especially in winter when temperatures reach −72°F (−40°C) and the wind is fierce. The saiga's unusual fleshy nose warms the air the animal breathes in, so the lungs do not become chilled. The bleak plains offer little cover, and so, as gazelles do, saigas rely on safety in numbers and speed to save them from predators such as wolves.

### DID YOU KNOW?

🐾 White fur is best at reflecting heat and so gazelles often stand with their white rump turned toward the sun.

🐾 A springbok can leap up to 10 feet into the air, from a standing start!

🐾 The gerenuk can survive without drinking water!

Despite its ungainly looks, the saiga is one of the fastest runners on Earth. It can sprint at up to 50 miles an hour over the flat plains—fast enough to outrun most predators. Saigas are hunted for their horns. So many animals have been killed that the species has already become extinct in many countries and is now listed as critically endangered.

◀ *Unlike other gazelles, the saiga has a large, fleshy snout. Saigas live in cold areas, and their unusual nose helps warm the air before it reaches the lungs.*

# GERBILS

The Mongolian gerbil is much loved as a pet all around
the world, but its wild cousins lead a much tougher life
in the deserts and dry grasslands of Africa and Asia.
Several species of gerbils are threatened with extinction.

Gerbils and their relatives, sand rats and jirds, are rodents. Most of these animals live in hot deserts or dry grasslands, where there is very little food and water and where predators, such as foxes, snakes, and birds of prey, are always on the lookout for an easy meal. These difficult conditions mean that gerbils have evolved some interesting features. To begin with, they hardly ever need to drink. There is a small amount of water in the seeds and roots they eat; gerbils manage to make this last by not sweating and producing just a few drops of urine a day. On hot days, gerbils stay in their burrows. Most species live in hot deserts, so they are active only at night.

## Avoiding Predators

After saving water, the next most important thing for gerbils is to avoid predators. A gerbil's fur provides excellent camouflage and usually matches the sand in the place where it lives. Some gerbils have a tuft of black fur at the end of the tail. This tuft stands out clearly when the gerbil moves and probably distracts predators, making them grab the gerbil's tail rather than its body. This gives the gerbil a chance to escape. Gerbils also use the tail tuft to sweep sand over their burrow entrance to hide it when they leave.

Many people keep Mongolian gerbils as pets. These small gerbils are agile and fun to watch. They make good pets because they are active during the day.

*The common brushtailed gerbil has large eyes and extremely long hind legs in comparison with its body size. So, it can see well and hop very quickly.*

### Fact File

**GERBILS**

**Family:** Muridae; subfamily Gerbillinae (95 species)

**Order:** Rodentia

**Where do they live?** Africa, the Middle East, and parts of Asia

Equator

**Habitat:** Deserts, savannas, and steppes; also on farmland

**Size:** Head–body length 2.5–8 inches (6–20 cm); weight 0.3–6.7 ounces (8–190 g)

**Coat:** Usually short golden, light brown, or grayish fur, paler on the belly

**Diet:** Mainly seeds, roots, and other plant material; some species eat insects, snails, and other small animals

**Breeding:** 1–12 offspring born after a gestation of 3–4 weeks; need constant care for first 2–3 weeks; weaned at around 4 weeks

**Life span:** 1–2 years

**Status:** Around one-quarter of species are threatened; 14 species are critically endangered

# GIANT PANDA

One of the world's most easily recognized mammals,
this gentle bear is a symbol of conservation worldwide.
Wild pandas live in such remote areas that many details
of their daily life are only just beginning to be understood.

**M**ost people will never see a giant panda in the wild, but these big black-and-white bears are still among the best loved of all mammals. They are the gentlest of bears. They are vegetarian, except for the occasional insect or other small animal that gets eaten with their favorite food, bamboo. It takes a lot of bamboo to feed a giant panda. A fully grown adult has to eat around 90 to 135 pounds of bamboo every day. That takes a long time—around ten to fourteen hours a day because every mouthful has to be well chewed before it is swallowed.

Giant pandas are extremely rare. They live in dense forests and do not like to be disturbed. Many of these forests have been cut down for timber or to make space for farms or human settlements. That loss of bamboo forest leaves giant pandas stranded in ever smaller patches of habitat. In addition, poachers hunt pandas for their fur coats. Some people are willing to pay a lot of money for the skin of such a rare animal even though it might make the pandas extinct.

## Breeding Pandas in Captivity

Worldwide, zoos are working together to build up the panda population. But breeding pandas in captivity is difficult, and the birth of new cubs is always a big event. Pandas seem to breed better in the wild. A cub develops fast and spends eighteen months learning survival skills from its mother before leaving to live alone.

*Sitting among the bamboo, this panda spends hours every day eating. These bears are endangered, and China has thirty-three preserves to help save them.*

## Fact File

### GIANT PANDA

***Ailuropoda melanoleuca***

**Family:** Ursidae

**Order:** Carnivora

**Where do they live?** Central and western China

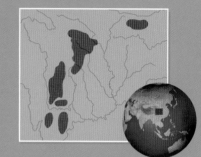

**Habitat:** Bamboo forests

**Size:** Head–body length 4–5 feet (120–150 cm); weight 220–330 pounds (100–150 kg)

**Coat:** Very thick fur; mostly white, with black legs and shoulders; black ear and eye patches

**Diet:** Bamboo and other grass, bulbs, and occasionally small animals

**Breeding:** 1–2 cubs born after 125–150 days' gestation; weaned at 8 months; mature at 5–6 years

**Life span:** 20 years in the wild, and 30 or more years in a zoo

**Status:** Endangered

# GIBBONS

Gibbons are well known for the spectacular way
in which they swing through the trees at full speed.
These apes also sing complicated and tuneful calls
that echo through their rain forest habitats.

Gibbons are apes, like orangutans, gorillas, chimpanzees, and humans. Gibbons are large, intelligent primates with complex social lives and no tail. Gibbons are forest animals—they spend almost their entire lives in the trees. They can move easily on two legs but can also get around by swinging from hand to hand below branches. Scientists call this way of moving brachiation, from the Latin word meaning "arm." Gibbons have long, strong arms and fingers. Short tendons in the arms ensure that when the gibbon's arm is outstretched, the fingers bend automatically to form a hook. So, a gibbon does not have to use muscle power to hang from a branch —it can dangle for hours without getting tired.

There are fourteen species of gibbons. Most species are about the same size, but the siamang grows almost twice as large as any other gibbon. Most species of gibbons live in different parts of Southeast Asia, and no one species overlaps with another. So, different species do not compete with each other for food.

## Filling Up on Fruit

Gibbons eat mainly fruit, which has to be ripe before they can digest it. Gibbons live only in the tropics, where ripe fruit is available all year round. Each gibbon knows its patch of forest very well and which trees bear fruit at different times. Even so, it can take a long time for a gibbon to find a good meal. Gibbons

*A common gibbon cradles her small baby. Also called lar or white-handed gibbons, they live in Thailand, the Malay Peninsula, and northern Sumatra.*

## Fact File

**GIBBONS**

**Family:** Hylobatidae (14 species)

**Order:** Primates

**Where do they live?** Southeast Asia, from eastern India to China and Borneo

Equator

**Habitat:** Forests

**Size:** Head–body length 18–35 inches (45–90 cm); weight 12–23 pounds (5.5–10.5 kg)

**Coat:** Medium to long fur, usually with distinctive patterns or ruff around face; color varies from white to black though various shades of gray, blonde, and brown

**Diet:** Fruit, leaves, and occasionally insects

**Breeding:** Single offspring born after 7–8 months' gestation

**Life span:** 25–30 years in the wild, and up to 40 years in a zoo

**Status:** Most species are declining in number; more than half are threatened with extinction

spend around three or four hours each day feeding and almost as long traveling through the trees in search of a tree bearing ripe fruit.

Several different types of trees depend on gibbons to carry their seeds far and wide. The gibbons eat the fruit, and the seeds pass through their gut and out of the other end with the droppings. Many seedlings only grow from seeds that have passed through a gibbon's gut. The seed covering is impenetrable to water until the digestive acids of the gut break it down. Some gibbons, especially the siamang, also eat leaves, particularly fresh new ones.

## Family Groups

Gibbons live in small family groups. Each group is started by a male and a female, who pair up as young adults and usually stay together for life. They rear just one offspring at a time, and it is usually at least two years before the next baby is born. Young gibbons stay with the family for six to eight years. After this time, they are

## MIXED COLORS

Most gibbon species look distinctive, with coat colors or markings that set them apart from others. In some species, even the males and females look quite different. For example, the black crested gibbon is named after the female, which is gold (right) and usually has a black crest. Male black crested gibbons are black with pale cheeks and are sometimes also known as white-cheeked gibbons.

often sing duets that echo for miles through the forest. Sometimes their offspring join in, too.

These songs let other gibbons in the area know that the territory is already occupied by strong, healthy gibbons and to stay away. Young adult males also sing to attract a mate. Because singing is hard work, a female can tell from a male's song whether he is strong and healthy.

Gibbons are threatened by habitat loss. Huge areas of rain forest in Southeast Asia have already been cut down for timber or cleared for farmland. All gibbon species are now much less common than they were twenty-five years ago; experts think that five species might even be extinct in another twenty years. The most endangered species are the island-dwelling Hainan gibbon and the silvery Javan gibbon.

fully grown and have learned everything they need to know to survive away from their parents. These gibbons are ready to move away and find a territory and a mate of their own.

### Rain Forest Songs and Habitat Loss

Calls and songs are extremely important to gibbons. Both males and female gibbons sing. Their songs include all sorts of long and short calls, many of which sound more like notes from a wind instrument than animal sounds. Pairs of gibbons

△ *A pair of silvery Javan gibbons scream together at their neighbors during a fierce dispute over territory.*

## DID YOU KNOW?

- The song of a gibbon can be heard up to 2 miles away!

- Gibbons hardly ever fall while swinging through the trees. Even if a branch breaks, they can usually twist in midair to grab another branch!

- A gibbon can leap up to 30 feet from tree to tree!

# GIRAFFE AND OKAPI

**Giraffes are unmistakable animals—they are world-famous symbols of the African plains. However, their cousin, the okapi, is so secretive and shy that it has only been known to science for little more than a century.**

Giraffes are the tallest living animals, and by a long way. The next tallest is the African elephant, which is around 6 feet shorter. A giraffe's legs account for around half of its height; its neck—the longest of any mammal—accounts for the rest. A giraffe's body is short and not particularly large—it is around the same size as that of a large cow.

## Browsing Giraffe Giants

Giraffes are browsers; they feed on the leaves and shoots of the trees that are scattered about the savanna grasslands where they live. There are plenty of other browsers on the savanna, including elephants and many different antelope. There is always stiff competition for food. The giraffe's amazingly long legs and neck allow it to feed from branches far above the heads of all the other browsers. That is a big advantage, especially in the dry season when there is not much fresh growth.

*Giraffes have large ears and eyes that help them hear and see well. They also have small horns on the top of their head and a long neck.*

## Fact File

### GIRAFFE AND OKAPI

**Family:** Giraffidae (2 species)

**Order:** Artiodactyla

**Where do they live?**
Giraffe—Africa south of the Sahara desert; okapi—central Africa

Equator

**Habitat:** Giraffe—wooded grasslands; okapi—dense tropical forests

**Size:** Giraffe—head–body length 12–15 feet (3.8–4.7 m); height 13–17 feet (3.9–5.3 m); weight 1,200–4,250 pounds (550–1,930 kg); okapi—head–body length 6–7 feet (190–200 cm); weight 465–550 pounds (210–250 kg)

**Coat:** Giraffe—short and neat, with distinctive pattern of dark brown to russet patches on cream, fawn, or gold background; okapi—short, glossy, mainly very rich dark brown coat, with bold white markings on legs and rump

**Diet:** Giraffe—leaves and shoots of savanna trees and shrubs; okapi—leaves

**Breeding:** Giraffe—single calf born after around 15 months' gestation; okapi—single calf born after 14–15 months' gestation

**Life span:** Giraffe—25 years in the wild, and 28 years in zoos; okapi—15 years or more

**Status:** Giraffe—lower risk, some local subspecies are threatened; okapi—near threatened

## Eating and Digesting

However, being so tall also has disadvantages. A giraffe's long legs make it difficult for the giraffe to reach the ground with its mouth. So, it cannot eat low-growing plants and struggles to drink. To reach the water, a giraffe has to spread its front legs extremely wide. From this awkward position, it can be difficult for a giraffe to react quickly to danger. In addition, giraffes struggle to move over uneven or boggy ground.

### DID YOU KNOW?

- The okapi was discovered by a British explorer only in 1901. It was the largest new mammal to be discovered in the twentieth century!

- A giraffe's tongue can be up to 18 inches long—and it is blue!

- Baby giraffes have horns that fold back so they do not get stuck when the animal is born!

- The structure of a giraffe's neck is similar to that of a crane on a building site!

*A giraffe's long neck enables it to reach the leaves and shoots that grow high in the trees. They do not have to compete for this food with shorter browsers.*

# WRESTLING MATCHES

From a young age, male giraffes spend a lot of time neck wrestling each other. To begin with this activity is just a game, but it also has a serious side. Neck wrestling helps strengthen the muscles of the neck and shoulders and also allows the males to size each other up. By the time a male reaches adulthood, he will know most of the other males in his area and know which one is the strongest. The largest and strongest males get to mate with more females, and the smaller males sensibly stay out of their way and wait until they grow larger.

Being so large means that giraffes must eat a lot and make the most of every mouthful of food. Leaves are difficult to digest, but giraffe digestion is thorough. Giraffes are ruminants. Between meals, giraffes chew the cud like cows: They cough food back up into their mouth and rechew it. That helps mash up the leaves and mix them with bacteria (single-celled microorganisms) from the giraffe's large stomach. These bacteria break down the tough molecules that make leaves difficult to digest. Unlike cows, giraffes can chew the cud while on the move in search of the next good feeding spot.

## Fighting for Females

Giraffes usually live in loose groups of mostly females and young giraffes; different members come and go and there is no fixed leader. Adult males wander alone but are never far away. There is no fixed breeding season, so the males are always on the lookout for females that are ready to breed. Females in season attract a lot of attention, and males compete for the right to mate by neck wrestling each other. These contests usually show who is the strongest, but if the males are closely matched, they may end up in a real fight. Fighting males kick with powerful

◯ *These two young giraffe bulls (males) are neck wrestling. They slowly intertwine their necks and push from one side to the other to find out which bull is strongest.*

hind legs and try to club each other with their hard, horny head. Giraffes also use their hooves to defend themselves against predators. But even adult giraffes are vulnerable to predators that hunt in teams, such as lions and hyenas. Giraffes use their height and good eyesight and hearing to check their surroundings for danger. Giraffes are safer in groups; lone giraffes are almost twice as likely to be attacked as giraffes in a group.

## Giraffe Relatives

Giraffes have an unlikely looking relative, called the okapi. An okapi

### DID YOU KNOW?

🐾 Despite its amazingly long neck, a giraffe has only seven neck bones—the same number as a human!

🐾 People once thought the giraffe looked like a cross between a camel and a leopard—hence its scientific name *camelopardalis*!

🐾 A male giraffe's skull gets thicker as it gets older. Its head gets heavier by around 2.2 pounds every year!

is roughly the size and shape of a horse and lives in the thick forests of central Africa in places where no giraffe could ever go. These two

🔻 *This okapi is searching for food in a thick rain forest. Okapis have zebralike stripes, especially on their hind legs.*

# SHRINKING RANGES

Giraffes once lived throughout most of southern Africa. Now their range is patchy, and they have disappeared from places where hunting, farming, and other human activities have developed. Some local varieties of western African giraffes are in danger of becoming extinct, and so the whole species is listed as conservation dependent. However, giraffes are one of the animals people on safari most like to see, and so it is in the interests of African countries to protect giraffes.

extremely different animals are a great example of how evolution can lead closely related animals to develop quite different features to cope with a variety of challenges.

Okapis are difficult to study in the wild, and much of what is known about them comes from studies in zoos. Even 100 years after they were discovered, there is still a lot people do not know about the natural behavior of okapis.

Okapis live alone for most of the time and are probably territorial. They feed like giraffes, on leaves stripped from branches by the teeth or plucked by the long tongue. Female okapis are in season for up to a month, which is much longer than for most other hoofed animals. That is probably because in the dense forest it can take males a long time to find females. Okapis are protected by law, but people still hunt them illegally for meat to eat or to sell.

*A giraffe mother stands tall over her calf. At birth, a giraffe weighs around 220 pounds and grows approximately 3 inches a month.*

# GOLDEN MOLES

In many ways, golden moles look and behave like ordinary moles but they have no visible eyes or ears. Even so, these burrowers can find their way about and track down prey in a complex system of underground tunnels.

Scientists once thought golden moles were close relatives of similar small insect eaters, such as true moles and hedgehogs. Now scientists have looked at the golden mole's genes and found that these animals are more closely related to aardvarks and elephants. A golden mole's closest cousin is the tenrec—a small, shrewlike or hedgehog-like African animal.

It is easy to see how golden moles got their name. They look very much like true moles and they live underground, burrowing through sandy soils in search of earthworms and insect grubs to eat. Their fur is short and velvety, with a metallic gold or bronze gleam.

## Shoving Aside Soil

Golden moles are powerful diggers. Their front legs are short but strong, and the wedge-shaped head is used to shove soil aside. The toes of the front feet have large claws, which are ideal for loosening hard-packed earth. Golden moles dig using a running motion, unlike true moles, which dig using a swimming action.

Golden moles live alone and spend almost their whole life underground. They dig feeding tunnels near the surface, where most prey can be found. Golden moles do not hunt—they simply patrol their tunnels and grab anything that comes their way. They sense the movement of prey as vibrations in the ground. Golden moles also dig deeper tunnels, in which they rest and rear their offspring.

*The smooth, outer hairs of the golden mole's coat are waterproof and so shiny that dirt does not stick. Clean fur helps keep the golden mole warm and dry.*

## Fact File

### GOLDEN MOLES

**Family:** Chrysochloridae (21 species)

**Order:** Afrosoricida

**Where do they live?** Southern Africa

Equator

**Habitat:** Sandy soils

**Size:** Head–body length 3–9 inches (7–23 cm); weight 0.5–5 ounces (15–142 g)

**Coat:** Short and neat; color varies with species; outer hairs have golden metallic gleam

**Diet:** Invertebrate grubs and small reptiles

**Breeding:** Litters of 1–2 offspring, born in rainy season

**Life span:** Not known

**Status:** Around half of all species are threatened with extinction

# GORILLAS

These primate powerhouses are the gentle giants of the great ape family, to which humans also belong. Gorillas are smart, sensitive, sociable experts in tropical forest survival, but there are few places where they are now able to live in peace.

People and gorillas have a lot in common. People are more closely related to gorillas than any other animal, except chimpanzees. Gorillas are massive, bulky animals—the largest of all primates. Male gorillas are larger and more muscular than females.

There are two species of gorillas, the eastern and the western. They look similar, but the eastern gorilla has a darker coat. Western gorillas live in tropical forests of the Congo basin in countries such as Congo and Equatorial Guinea as well as Nigeria and Cameroon. Eastern gorillas live in swampy and mountainous forests of Rwanda and Uganda in Africa.

Gorillas need a lot of food. They love fruit and eat as much as they can find. They fill up on leaves and shoots and other plant material. All of this food takes a lot of grinding, so gorillas have massive cheek teeth and huge jaw muscles that help them chew. These muscles give the face a distinctive deep and wide shape.

## Ground-living Gorillas

Gorillas walk on all fours, on the soles of the feet and the knuckles of the hands. Their arms are at least as long and as strong as their legs. Gorillas do not travel long distances—rarely more than a few hundred yards a day. Usually a troop (group) can find everything it needs to survive within just a few square miles, and gorillas are not territorial. Gorillas spend most of their days on the ground, but they can climb well, too. Small

*An old silverback lowland gorilla casts a quizzical eye over his family group. A silverback is a fully grown male in charge of a group of females and young.*

## Fact File

**GORILLAS**

*Gorilla gorilla* and *Gorilla beringei*

**Family:** Hominidae

**Order:** Primates

**Where do they live?** Africa, close to the equator

Equator

**Habitat:** Tropical forests

**Size:** Height 50–71 inches (130–180 cm); weight 200–400 pounds (90–180 kg)

**Coat:** Dark brownish gray to black, short on back, shaggy elsewhere; large males have patch of gray fur on the back

**Diet:** Leaves, fruit, shoots, bark, and a few invertebrates, such as termites and caterpillars

**Breeding:** Single offspring (twins rare), born after 250–270 days' gestation; weaned at 2–3 years; mature at 8–10 years

**Life span:** 35 years in the wild, and 50 years in zoos

**Status:** Both species endangered; some subspecies are critically endangered

gorillas are nimble and can swing from their arms, as gibbons do. Gorillas climb trees to pick fruit and to rest. When sleeping in trees, gorillas build a nest from folded branches. Sleeping in a nest is warmer and safer than lying on the cold, damp, and steep ground.

## Groups of Gorillas

Gorilla groups are extremely stable. Eastern gorilla groups may contain forty animals, but ten is more normal. Groups of western gorillas contain five to ten animals. Western gorillas eat more fruit, and as ripe trees are scattered around the forest, it is easier for them to feed in small groups. Eastern gorillas eat mostly leaves, which are always easy to find.

Each group is led by one massive male, who protects several adult females and their offspring. Young gorillas have a long childhood. Many gorillas are not weaned until they are three years old and stay with their mother for ten years or more. By this time, they have one or even two younger brothers or sisters. Each gorilla knows all the other group members, and the adult females are often related. When they reach adulthood, most young gorillas move away from their mother's group. Young females join up with another group to breed. Females do not wander alone, so they wait until their group comes close to another and simply swap groups.

*A female gorilla and her infants rest in the middle of the day after spending the morning feeding.*

# WHAT FUTURE FOR GORILLAS?

Gorillas are highly endangered. They have lost huge areas of habitat due to human activities such as hunting, logging, farming, and building. The countries where they live are poor and many have suffered long wars. When people themselves are fighting to survive, it is difficult for them to show much concern for gorillas. However, in countries where there is peace, there is also hope for the gorillas' future. Tourists come from all over the world to see gorillas, and the money they spend can make a big difference to the whole country.

Young males usually join groups of other males and spend a few years growing big and strong. One day they may lead their own group. A powerful male of fifteen to twenty years can move in when an old male dies or becomes too weak to look after his females. If the females like the new male, they stay with him.

## DID YOU KNOW?

- Gorillas share 98 percent of their DNA with chimpanzees and humans. Gorillas, chimps, and humans are all equal cousins!

- Gorillas have the language skills of an average two-year-old child!

- Gorillas weigh as much as two or three adult humans!

# GRAY WHALE

Gray whales are long-distance travelers, feeding in the far north and breeding in the tropics. Every year gray whales migrate more than 12,000 miles. Because they nearly always travel in sight of land, these whales are easy to watch.

Gray whales are a fairly common sight along the west coast of North America. In spring and fall, thousands of people travel there every year to see gray whales pass by on their long migrations. However, fifty years ago, these huge mammals were almost extinct. They had been hunted for hundreds of years for meat and oil. The gray whale population had fallen to just a few thousand individuals. Now they are protected, and the only people allowed to hunt gray whales are Inuits and Native Americans, who use traditional methods and kill only a few whales each year. There are now around 25,000 gray whales living in the eastern Pacific Ocean.

Gray whales are a distinctive shape. Instead of a dorsal (back) fin, gray whales have a row of bumps running along the lower part of the back. In adults, the skin is always blotchy and covered with big clumps of barnacles.

## Winter Feeding, Summer Breeding

Female gray whales are pregnant for thirteen months and rear only one calf every other year. Female gray whales mate one winter, give birth during the next winter, and mate again during the third winter. Newborn gray whales are much skinnier than adults. It takes the calf a few months to build up a thick enough layer of blubber, or fat, to cope with living in cold water. So, the mother must travel somewhere warm to give birth. That is why gray whales gather every winter in the warm, shallow waters of Baja California, off the coast of Mexico.

*A big, barnacled gray whale breaching. A breach takes place when a whale leaps halfway or more out of the water and then falls back onto its side.*

## Fact File

### GRAY WHALE

*Eschrichtius robustus*
**Family:** Eschrichtidae
**Order:** Cetacea

**Where do they live?** Coastal areas of Pacific Ocean, from Baja California and Japan, to arctic waters

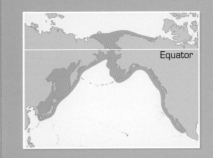

Equator

**Habitat:** Coastal waters less than 330 feet (100 m) deep

**Size:** Head–body length 39–50 feet (12–15 m); weight 18–38 tons (16–34 metric tons)

**Skin:** Mottled gray, with patches of barnacles and whale lice

**Diet:** Plankton and bottom-living invertebrates, mostly small crustaceans

**Breeding:** Single calf born after 13 months' gestation; weaned at 7 months; able to breed at around 8 years

**Life span:** Up to 77 years

**Status:** No longer hunted intensively, but still conservation dependent; the population around Japan is critically endangered

# GRAY WHALE

**1**

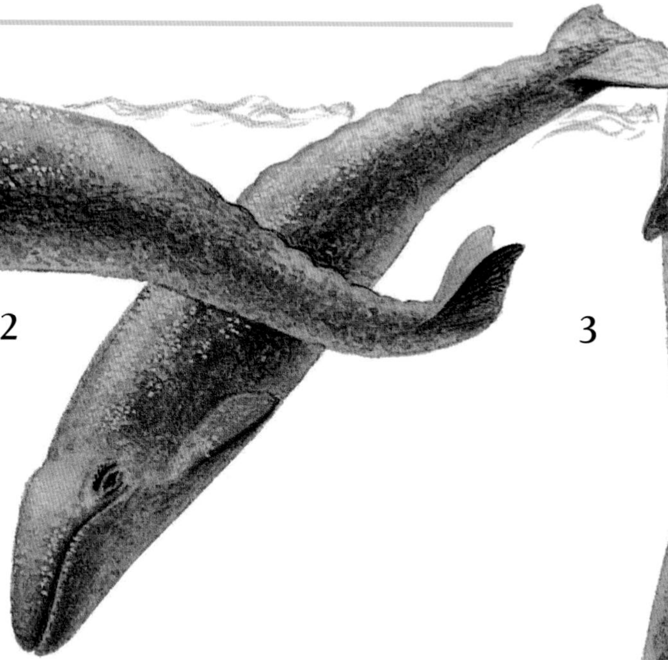

**2**

**3**

1 *A gray whale blows after a dive.*

2 *When a gray whale prepares to make a deep dive, its tail flukes appear above the water.*

3 *A gray whale spy-hops, sticking its head above the water to check its surroundings.*

4 *A gray whale mother swims with her calf.*

Males and nonpregnant females also mate in the warm water. Then all the gray whales return north to cold waters in the spring.

Gray whale calves grow amazingly fast—the mother's milk is extremely fattening and a calf can put on up to 70 pounds a day. By the time the calves reach arctic waters, at around six or seven months old,

they are fat enough to survive the cold and ready to begin eating solid food.

Gray whales eat mainly small, flealike crustaceans called amphipods. In midsummer, billions of these creatures are present; the long hours of daylight encourage the algae and other plankton (microscopic animals and plantlike life-forms) on which amphipods feed to grow and reproduce superfast.

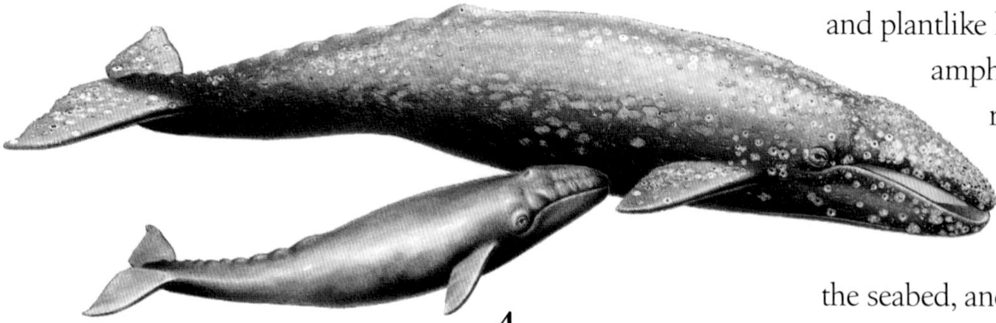

## Sieve Eaters

Amphipods live in the seabed, and gray whales have an unusual way of feeding. The whales swim to the seafloor and plow along

**4**

the bottom with their mouth open. They take in lots of mud and sand, along with the amphipods and other small buried animals. Instead of teeth, gray whales have a mouth full of bristly combs, called baleen. Baleen acts as a sieve to collect the food, while the mud and sand pass through the baleen with the water and leave the mouth. From above,

*Gray whales often swim within half a mile of shore, which makes them easy to watch closely.*

feeding gray whales are easy to spot because they create clouds of stirred-up mud from the ocean floor and leave long furrows in the seabed.

Having fed well all summer, adult whales return to Baja California in the fall. Males and females whose calves have just weaned go there to mate. Once the females are pregnant, the gray whales quickly travel north to begin feeding again.

## WHALE WATCHING

Gray whales are curious animals. They often swim toward boats and seem interested in people. Some gray whales come right alongside small boats and even allow themselves to be stroked. Being so trusting and inquisitive once made gray whales easy targets for hunters. Now gray whales are protected, and the boats that go out in search of them are full of whale watchers instead of hunters.

### Hunted by Killer Whales

Apart from humans, the only other animals that hunt gray whales are killer whales, or orcas. Orcas hunt in groups and target young calves. The gray whale mother can do very little to protect her calf once orcas begin an attack. Gray whale calves cannot swim fast enough to get away, but sometimes they can hide from orcas in dense patches of seaweed.

# HAMSTERS

Most people in the western world know these small rodents with their bulging cheek pouches as pets. However, in much of Asia and eastern Europe, hamsters are wild animals. Some species are farm pests, while others are now very rare.

The most popular species of pet hamster is the golden hamster, but this species is extremely rare in the wild and lives only in a tiny area of Syria in the Middle East. Most pet golden hamsters are descended from just one female, one of four young hamsters taken from the wild in 1930. There are twenty-six species of wild hamsters. Not all hamsters are small; some species are almost the size of a rabbit. Hamsters live mainly in dry habitats, and some even live in deserts. They are active mostly at night, when they can avoid overheating and stay out of the way of predators.

## Hamster Hoarders

Hamsters eat mainly grains, seeds, shoots, and roots. They are great hoarders. They have large cheek pouches, into which they can stuff dozens of seeds to carry back their burrows and store in underground larders. Hamsters hibernate in winter but wake up from time to time to feed from their larder. Common hamsters also sometimes add meat to their diet, by hunting insects, small lizards, and mice.

Despite their reputation as cute pets, wild hamsters can be fierce; they live alone and do not like company. Males fight when they meet, and the large Korean hamster even attacks dogs or people in self-defense.

Hamsters breed fast. Females breed at less than two months old. Litters are large; up to twenty-two offspring in the Korean gray hamster, but usually around ten.

*A white Russian hamster bites into a peanut. Hamsters are rodents. All rodents have two pairs of sharp incisor teeth, which grow throughout life.*

### Fact File

**HAMSTERS**

**Family:** Muridae; subfamilies Cricetinae and Calomyscinae (26 species)

**Order:** Rodentia

**Where do they live?** Europe and temperate Asia

Equator

**Habitat:** Dry landscapes, including grasslands, deserts, mountain slopes, and farmland

**Size:** Head–body length 2–11 inches (5–28 cm); weight 1.8–32 ounces (50–900 g)

**Coat:** Soft and thick; usually gold, brown, or gray; paler on the belly, with variable markings

**Diet:** Mainly seeds, shoots, and roots

**Breeding:** Litters of several offspring (up to 22) born after 15–37 days' gestation

**Life span:** 2–3 years

**Status:** 2 species are endangered; 1 species is vulnerable

# HEDGEHOGS AND MOONRATS

**Spiny hedgehogs are familiar to most people living in Europe, Asia, and Africa. Their cousins, the moonrats and gymnures of South Asia, are much more secretive and less well known.**

Hedgehogs are popular animals, especially with gardeners, because they eat a lot of small pests such as slugs and beetle grubs, which damage plants. Hedgehogs are also easy to watch. With their coat of prickly spines for protection, they do not run away when frightened—they simply roll into a ball and rely on their spines for protection. In time, hedgehogs can become quite tame. Many people put out food for hedgehogs, which come to eat in plain view.

The best-known hedgehog is the common Eurasian hedgehog. Fifteen other hedgehog species live in different parts of Asia and Africa, many in deserts. Moonrats and gymnures look a little like nonspiny hedgehogs. They are nocturnal (active at night) and eat invertebrates (animals without backbones), but the details of their lives are not well known.

## Hunters and Hibernators

Hedgehogs have small, bright eyes and a long, pointed snout. They hunt mainly by smell. They are active at night and travel long distances in search of food. Hedgehogs can climb and swim well, and they also have excellent hearing. In winter, when food is scarce and temperatures are low, the common hedgehog hibernates in a nest made of leaves. Hedgehogs from warm climates do not need to hibernate.

Hedgehogs have only two serious enemies: badgers, which can easily kill them, and people driving cars.

*Although a hedgehog's spines protect it against most predators, they are no defense against lawnmowers or cars, which kill millions of hedgehogs every year.*

## Fact File

### HEDGEHOGS AND MOONRATS

**Family:** Erinaceidae (16 species of hedgehogs; 8 species of moonrats)

**Order:** Erinaceidae

**Where do they live?** Europe, Africa, and most of Asia, including Indonesia; hedgehogs imported as pets into North America

Equator

**Habitat:** Woodlands, grasslands, forests, mangroves, farmland, and urban parks and backyards

**Size:** Head–body length 4–18 inches (10–45 cm); weight 0.5–70 ounces (15–2,000 g)

**Coat:** Moonrats—coarse hair; hedgehogs—modified hairs form sharp spines

**Diet:** Worms, snails, slugs, beetles and other insects, birds' eggs, and carrion (meat of dead animals)

**Breeding:** Litters of offspring born after 30–48 days' gestation

**Life span:** Up to 7 years

**Status:** 7 species are at risk

# HIPPOPOTAMUSES

Common hippos are among the largest hoofed animals. They spend half of their life wallowing in shallow water and mud and eat only grass. But despite this relaxed, vegetarian lifestyle, hippos have a reputation for being bad tempered and extremely dangerous.

There are two species (types) of hippopotamuses—the common hippo and the pygmy hippo. Common hippopotamuses lead a double life. By day they gather in rivers and pools, where they wallow and doze and often squabble among themselves. Each evening they come out onto dry land to feed. Common hippos eat grass and travel several miles to find good grazing. At dawn they walk back to the water. There are many advantages to living in water that make all the coming and going worthwhile. Hippos have no fur and their skin is thin. The skin dries out fast, and if a hippo spends too much time out of water in the sun, its skin burns and then dries out and cracks.

## Wallowing in Water

Spending the day in water also prevents hippos from overheating, but the water is warm enough that they never become chilled. As the water supports most of the hippo's body weight, it does not have to

*While it wallows in the water, this common hippopotamus shows off two razor-sharp tusks in its lower jaw as it opens its mouth wide.*

## Fact File

### HIPPOPOTAMUSES

**Family:** Hippopotamidae (2 species)

**Order:** Artiodactyla

**Where do they live?**
Common hippo—Africa, south of the Sahara desert; pygmy hippo—West Africa

Equator

**Habitat:** Common hippopotamus—pools and slow-moving rivers, close to good grazing; pygmy hippopotamus—dense tropical forests

**Size:** Common hippo—head–body length 10 feet 9 inches–11 feet 4 inches (3.4–3.45 m), weight 1.6–3.6 tons (1.4–3.2 metric tons); pygmy hippo—head–body length 4 feet 11 inches–5 feet 8 inches (1.5–1.75 m), weight 400–600 pounds (180–275 kg)

**Skin:** Common hippo—bluish gray, mottled with pink, almost completely hairless; pygmy hippo—oily, olive-green to gray, and hairless

**Diet:** Common hippo—grass; pygmy hippo—fruit, shoots, ferns, grass, and herbs

**Breeding:** Common hippo—single calf born after 240 days' gestation; pygmy hippo—single calf born after 190–210 days' gestation; both weaned at 12 months, mature at 8 years

**Life span:** Common hippo—45 years in the wild, and 49 years in zoos; pygmy hippo—35 years in the wild, and 42 years in zoos

**Status:** Common hippo—not threatened, but numbers declining, and 1 subspecies (local type) vulnerable; pygmy hippo—vulnerable, Niger Delta subspecies is critically endangered

spend much energy during the day. That is just as well, because a hippo's grassy diet would not provide enough energy to fuel its large body if it had to keep warm or move about on land.

The hippo's body is large and barrel shaped and the legs are short. The hippo has webbed toes that help it swim. The head is large, too, with the eyes, ears, and nostrils arranged on the top of the head and snout. So, a hippo can see, hear, and breathe while wallowing low in the water.

A hippo's mouth is huge. A hippo can open its mouth extremely wide to form an enormous yawning gape, showing two long, razor-sharp tusks in the lower jaw. These teeth are not used for feeding—they are weapons. Hippos are aggressive, and fights are common, especially between males.

## Territorial Behavior

Each large male hippo marks out a section of riverbank as a territory by scattering dung all over it. Males mate with the females in their territory. Mating happens in the water and is over quickly. At other times, males and females ignore each other. Large males allow other males to use the same section of river, providing they do not mate with the females living there.

Hippopotamus calves are born in the water and stay close to their mother for safety. When the river is crowded with hippopotamuses, the calves can easily be crushed or drowned. Calves suckle underwater and remain under the mother's watchful eye long after they are weaned and until they are ready to breed, at around eight years old.

*A group of common hippos wallows by the edge of a river. When it gets too hot, they enter the water to cool off.*

## SWEATING BLOOD?

People used to think that hippos sweated blood. However, they produce a pink, oily substance from the skin, which acts as a moisturizer and sunscreen. That helps keep their skin in good condition. It may also stop germs from infecting the animal. Hippos often get cuts and scrapes from rocks in the water or from fights. However, although hippos live in filthy water, their wounds hardly ever seem to get infected.

*This pygmy hippopotamus has found something to eat. These hippos eat fruit, shoots, ferns, grass, and herbs, while the common hippopotamus eats only grass.*

### Pygmy Hippopotamuses

The life of the pygmy hippo is very different. These shy forest animals usually live alone, except for mothers with a calf. They mate in the water, as do common hippos, and wallow in mud or water to cool down. Pygmy hippos spend much more time on dry land, however. The sun is less of a problem because their skin is oily and shiny and does not dry out as fast as that of common hippos. Pygmy hippos also live under the shade of trees and sometimes even use large burrows dug by other animals.

Pygmy hippos are difficult to study. Many scientists fear they are becoming rare. Pygmy hippos are sometimes hunted for meat, but the main problem is loss of habitat. Large areas of forests in West Africa continue to be cut down for timber and to make space for farming.

### DID YOU KNOW?

The word *hippopotamus* means "river horse" in Greek.

Hippos are bad tempered, and African people consider them among the most dangerous of all wild animals!

Compared with hippos, humans have tough skin. Human skin is much thicker than that of a hippopotamus and loses water at about a quarter of the speed.

# HONEY POSSUM

**This tiny, mouselike marsupial has no close living relatives—and some people think it should not be called a possum at all. Honey possums are among the very few mammals that eat only pollen and nectar.**

Honey possums are marsupials, so females rear their offspring in a pouch, but they also have a grasping tail like a harvest mouse and nimble fingers like a tiny monkey. Honey possums eat only nectar and pollen, just as a hummingbird does. Honey possums collect their food from flowers using a long tongue that has a brushlike tip. They have just a few tiny, peglike teeth and cannot chew other types of food. In winter, if food is difficult to find, honey possums go into a deep sleep to save energy. This sleep is a little like hibernation, but it lasts for only a few days.

## Agile Climbers

Honey possums are agile climbers and, as they weigh so little, they can climb onto extremely fine branches to reach the flowers. They have tiny, monkeylike hands and feet, and the tips of their fingers and toes are wide, which allows them to grip well. The long tail can curl around branches. A honey possum can even dangle from its tail because it grips so tightly.

Female honey possums are larger than males and more territorial. They can breed at any time of the year. Their babies are the smallest of any mammal, weighing only a tiny fraction of an ounce. These tiny creatures crawl to the mother's pouch and attach themselves to a teat. Baby honey possums grow fast, increasing their weight to around 0.1 ounce in two months, and then begin exploring the outside world.

*A honey possum has found two flowers to feed on. These tiny marsupials are unusual mammals because they eat only flower pollen and nectar.*

## Fact File

**HONEY POSSUM**

*Tarsipes rostratus*

**Family:** Tarsipedidae

**Order:** Diprotodontia

**Where do they live?:** Southwestern Australia

Equator

**Habitat:** Heathlands and open scrubby woodlands

**Size:** Head–body length 2.6–3.5 inches (6.5–9 cm); weight 0.3–0.6 ounce (7–16 g)

**Coat:** Grayish brown, tinged with orange on flanks; three dark stripes along back

**Diet:** Nectar and pollen

**Breeding:** 2–3 offspring born after around 28 days' gestation; weaned at 10 weeks; mature at 10 months

**Life span:** Less then 2 years

**Status:** Lower risk; depends on food supply

# HOOFED MAMMALS

**Four out of five of Earth's large land mammals have fingernails and toenails that grow into hard, strong hooves. These animals come in a huge variety of shapes and sizes. Most hoofed mammals are fleet-footed vegetarians, and several have become vital to people as farm animals.**

**M**ost hoofed mammals have a stout, barrel-shaped body, a longish neck and a long, narrow head. They have thick skin, and their coats range from short and silky in most antelope and horses, to long and shaggy in the yak, woolly in sheep and camels, sparse and bristly in pigs, and nonexistent in hippopotamuses and rhinoceroses. Several groups of hoofed mammals have horns, and in most deer, the males grow a fresh set of antlers every year. The legs of hoofed animals are slim and usually quite long. Their feet have fewer than five toes, and the bones of the foot are longer than in other mammals.

There are two main groups of hoofed mammals: odd-toed and even-toed ungulates. Odd-toed ungulates have an odd number of toes on each foot. They include horses, which

have one toe, and tapirs and rhinoceroses, which have three toes on each foot. Even-toed ungulates form a larger group, including cattle, deer, pigs, hippopotamuses, and camels. Even-toed ungulates have feet with two or four toes.

The structure of a hoofed mammal's foot is ideal for running, but not much use for anything else. Horses, pigs, and deer can never

1. *Black rhinoceros*
2. *Mountain tapir*
3. *African ass*

🔵 *The American bison is an enormous hoofed mammal that now lives mostly in parks and refuges.*

use their feet for grasping. Some hoofed mammals use their feet as weapons for kicking or stamping or as tools for digging shallow holes. However, apart from that, the most any of these mammals can manage is an awkward scratch of the belly with a hind foot. Some hoofed mammals can use other body parts for more delicate operations. For example, the black rhinoceros can pluck individual leaves with its upper lip, a giraffe can grip branches and clean around its own eyes using its very long tongue, and horses can flick away flies with their tail.

## Plant Eaters All

All hoofed mammals eat plants. Some of these mammals are specialized, such as the common hippopotamus and the white rhinoceros, which eat only grass. Others, such as giraffes and deer, eat a variety of leaves and shoots from many different kinds of plants. A few, including pigs and peccaries, eat anything from fruit and roots, to fungi and the flesh of other animals.

## Fact File

### HOOFED MAMMALS

**Families:** 13 families (212 species)

**Orders:** Perissodactyla and Artiodactyla

**ODD-TOED UNGULATES (Perissodactyla)**

**Horses, zebras, and asses:** 7 species of large, fast-running grazers, with a single toe and hoof on each foot

**Tapirs:** 4 species of medium-to-large, stout-bodied, slim-legged mammals of tropical forests

**Rhinoceroses:** 5 species of large, thick-skinned, three-toed herbivores; most have large horns growing from the snout

### EVEN-TOED UNGULATES (Artiodactyla)

**Pigs:** 13 species of medium-to-large omnivorous forest animals with a robust body and slim legs

**Peccaries:** 3 species of South American, piglike mammals

**Hippopotamuses:** 2 species of large, barrel-bodied, partly aquatic African mammals

**Camels and llamas:** 6 species of medium-to-large desert- or mountain-dwelling mammals with long legs, a long neck, and woolly fur

**Deer:** At least 38 species of medium-to-large, herbivores with cloven (split) hooves; most have long legs; males bear antlers or tusks

**Giraffe and okapi:** 2 species of horned African browsing mammals, one a tall plains dweller, the other a shy forest mammal

**Cattle, antelope, and sheep:** At least 123 species of cloven-hoofed, often horned, ruminants; several species are domesticated

However, plants make up most of the diet for nearly all types of hoofed mammals.

Some plants are better food than others, but the best ones are nearly always the hardest to find. Fruit, for example, contains lots of energy and is easy to digest. However, it grows only on certain plants and at certain times of the year. As a result, no hoofed mammals rely completely on fruit. New leaves and shoots and flesh grass are tender enough to digest quite easily, but in some

## DID YOU KNOW?

🐾 The saola is a small ox that lives in the region around the Laos–Vietnam border. It is so secretive that it was only discovered by scientists in 1992.

🐾 The largest land mammal that ever lived was a 13.3-ton rhinoceros called *Indricotherium*. It is now extinct.

🐾 Africa is home to the greatest number of different species of hoofed mammals.

◀ *A pair of male hippopotamuses fight over the right to mate with females, using their razor-sharp lower canines.*

▶ *A wild boar looks for food. These hoofed mammals live in Europe, northern Africa, Asia, Sumatra, Japan, and Taiwan. They have also been introduced to North America.*

A red deer stag displays its large antlers. Most male deer grow a set of antlers every year and use them to fight for territory and access to females.

ruminants, have evolved a way to make use of really tough plant matter. They have a slow, complicated type of digestion that allows them to make the most of every mouthful of grass, leaves, or even wood. Ruminant animals include cattle, antelope, deer, giraffes, chevrotains, and musk deer. They all have a many-chambered stomach that contains bacteria. These single-celled microorganisms help break down the tough plant molecules and turn them into simple chemicals that can be digested. Horses and rhinoceroses also use bacteria to help them break down plant matter. In these animals, however, the bacteria live near the end of the gut in an organ called the cecum.

parts of the world, these plants grow only in spring and summer. Tough old grass, bark, and older leaves are nearly always easy to find, but they are the hardest of all to digest. Different species of hoofed mammals have evolved to eat a variety of food types. One group, known as

## MAKING FACES

Apart from the nose, most hoofed mammals have a second scent organ in the mouth, called Jacobson's organ. Male hoofed mammals, such as the Asiatic ass (right), often use this organ to "taste" the scent of a female to see if she is ready to breed. The males usually make a strange face when they are doing this, with their lips curled back. Scientists call this behavior the flehmen response.

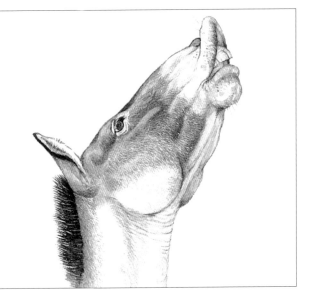

## DOMESTICATING HOOFED MAMMALS

People began to domesticate (breed and tame) animals, such as cattle, sheep, horses, and camels, around 10,000 years ago. Farming these animals is easier than hunting them, and by controlling the way they breed, farmers have been able to develop new breeds—cows that produce more milk or better meat, sheep with better wool, stronger horses, and so on. The wild ancestors of many domesticated hoofed mammals are all but extinct.

◀ *Free-roaming mustangs of North America are descended from escaped domesticated horses.*

Food passes through the gut of rhinoceroses and horses much more quickly. These animals can afford to eat lower-quality food, as long as they get plenty of it.

### Danger from Predators

Most hoofed animals have good eyesight and hearing, which they use mainly for sensing danger from predators and picking up signals from other members of their species. The sense of smell is also extremely important to most hoofed mammals. Those animals that live in dry areas rely on the occasional rainstorm to encourage the growth of fresh leaves and grass. They can pick up the scent of rain from miles away, and they flock toward it. In Africa, rains can bring vast herds of antelope, zebra, and cattle from hundreds of miles around to create an amazing sight on the open plains.

Smell can be vital in warning of predators nearby, and it is one of the most important senses for communication. Most hoofed mammals, especially even-toed ones, have glands in the face and feet that produce scent. They leave this scent on the ground, on objects such as trees and rocks, or even on each other. The scent tells other animals a great deal about the animal that left it— how old it is, whether it is male or female, its health, and whether it is ready to breed. Some hoofed mammals, in particular horses, also use sound and body language to communicate with others of the same species.

## Social Lives

The social lives of hoofed mammals vary. Those that live in the open, including most grazers, live either in large groups for safety, such as zebras, South American guanacos, and gazelles,

or they develop impressive defenses, such as the large size and fearsome horns of the African rhinoceros. Forest-dwelling hoofed mammals such as small deer, pigs, and okapis, live alone or in small groups.

## DID YOU KNOW?

🐾 The American pronghorn is the fastest living hoofed mammal— it can reach speeds up to 53 miles per hour!

🐾 The smallest hoofed mammal is the lesser mouse deer, or chevrotain, which weighs little more than 2 pounds, around the same as a standard bag of sugar!

🐾 The milk produced by female Himalayan yaks is pink!

1. *Male mule deer*
2. *Saola*
3. *Male ibex*

# HORSES, ZEBRAS, AND ASSES

For many people, wild horses are a symbol of grace
and freedom. Their close relatives, zebras, are equally
admired for their exotic coat patterns, and asses
are perhaps the fastest and hardiest of the group.

Horses and their relatives appeared around fifty million years ago in North America. The first horses were small forest animals with three hoofed toes on each foot. They adapted to eating grass and began to live on the plains. However, it was dangerous for small, plant-eating animals to live out in the open. So, horses gradually became larger and superb runners to escape predators. Their legs grew long and slim, and their two side toes shrank away. That left one large toe, which made the foot bones much less flexible but extremely light and strong. Horses have speed, strength, and stamina. They can sprint at up to 50 miles an hour or travel all day at a steady canter.

## Grazing Days

Grass is difficult to digest, especially without a large, complex stomach like that of cattle and sheep. Horses have only a simple stomach, so the grass they eat passes through quickly. Horse dung contains a lot of undigested grass. To make up for this waste, horses eat a lot of grass. They crop the grass with their large front teeth and grind it up with their large cheek teeth. These teeth have ridges of enamel that help shred and pulp the grass before it is swallowed.

Horses spend most of their days grazing. They feed standing up and can react quickly if they sense danger. A horse can relax and even snooze without having to lie down. When feeding, a horse or zebra raises its head

*Closely related to horses and asses, zebras are instantly recognized because of their distinctive black-and-white stripes. They live only in Africa.*

## Fact File

### HORSES, ZEBRAS, AND ASSES

**Family:** Equidae (7 species)

**Order:** Artiodactyla

**Where do they live?** Eastern Africa, the Middle East, and Central Asia

Equator

**Habitat:** Savanna and steppe grasslands and deserts

**Size:** Head–body length 6 feet 6 inches–9 feet (200–275 cm); weight 560–890 pounds (255–405 kg)— 2,860 pounds (1,300 kg) in domestic horse

**Coat:** Short and neat to slightly shaggy; varies from pale gray or fawn to black; zebras and asses have stripes; long-haired mane and tail tuft

**Diet:** Grass and other plant material

**Breeding:** 1 foal, sometimes twins; 11–14 months' gestation; weaned at 9–24 months; mature at 2–4 years

**Life span:** 25–45 years

**Status:** True horses officially extinct in wild, but millions live in captivity; African ass critically endangered; Asiatic ass, mountain zebra, and Grevy's zebra endangered

**1**

1 A male Przewalski's horse displays the stallion's bite threat. These horses are like the ancestors of all domestic horses.

2 A female African ass shows the kick threat, with its ears held back.

3 A male onager, a subspecies (local type) of the Asiatic ass, creates a pile of dung to mark its territory.

## DID YOU KNOW?

The word *mustang* comes from the Spanish word *mesteno*, which means "belonging to nobody."

Horses were extinct in America until the sixteenth century, when Spanish settlers took them back to their ancestral home.

A horse reveals its mood by changes in its ear, mouth, and tail positions!

**2**

**3**

## WHY ARE ZEBRAS STRIPY?

People used to think that the stripy coat of zebras was a type of camouflage or a way to confuse predators. Now scientists think that all horses were once stripy and that zebras kept their stripes because they help keep members of the herd together—zebras are attracted to each other's eye-catching patterns. Other horses and asses have mostly lost their stripes, although some still have faint markings on their legs.

often to check the surroundings, always alert. Even when a horse's head is down, its ears move this way and that, checking for danger.

Horses have good eyesight and hearing, but their sense of smell is not as good as that of many other hoofed animals. In the open, sound travels a long way, and it is usually easy to see what is going on, so horses use mostly sounds and body language to communicate.

### Herding and Mating

Adult female horses, zebras, and asses live in herds. The females are called mares. In wild horses and plains zebras, each herd is led by an adult male, or stallion. The stallion guards his mares from other males and predators. In asses and Grevy's zebras, the stallion protects a territory. He claims the right to mate with mares that wander into his patch but does not prevent them from leaving if they choose to go. The

△ *Each zebra has a unique pattern of black-and-white stripes.*

stallion that manages to hold onto the best territory is the most successful at mating because the mares spend more time with him.

Female horses come into season (are ready to mate) soon after giving birth. They are pregnant for a year or more. This long gestation ensures that when the foal arrives, it is well developed. A young foal can stand within minutes of being born and run within hours. That is important because, living in the open, there is nowhere to hide. A young horse or ass that cannot keep up with the herd will be easily picked off by a predator.

## DID YOU KNOW?

- There are now around 2,000 Przewalski's horses alive. Most of them live in zoos and wildife reserves.
- Przewalski's horses were named after a Polish explorer who served in the Russian army in the nineteenth century!
- The Romans called zebras hippotigres, or "tiger horses," because of their stripes!

## Going Wild

Some domesticated horses and ponies have returned to the wild. In North America, herds of mustangs live wild on the plains and in the

*The African ass lives only in a thin strip of northeastern Africa. It is now critically endangered.*

## MULES, HINNEYS, AND OTHER MIX-UPS

Since horses, asses, and zebras are closely related, they can sometimes breed with each other to produce hybrids. The most common hybrid is a cross between a female horse and male ass. The result is a mule (right). If the cross is between a male horse and a female ass, the hybrid is a hinney. Mules are more useful to people than hinneys because they are stronger. Zebras can also be crossed with horses to produce hybrids known as zorses.

mountains. In Europe, there are also feral horses and ponies in France and the United Kingdom. In Australia, where horses have never lived naturally, domestic horses have escaped or were set free by European settlers. These horses now have around 200,000 wild descendants, known as brumbies. That is the world's largest population of feral horses, or horses that were once domesticated but have since gone wild.

### All At Risk

Of the seven species of horses, zebras, and asses, all but the plains zebra and domestic horse are at risk of becoming extinct. Przewalski's horses became extinct in the wild in 1969. Since then, zoos have been breeding these horses, and some have been returned to the wild in Mongolia. The next most threatened species is the African ass, which is critically endangered. Grevy's zebra, the mountain zebra, and the Asiatic ass are also endangered.

*Mules are usually sterile— they cannot produce foals. Although a mule's ears are longer than the horse parent's, they are the same shape.*

# HYRAXES

**Hyraxes look like large rodents, but they are more closely related to elephants. Hyraxes are sturdy, small- to medium-sized mammals, with short legs, a stumpy tail, and a small, pointed face.**

Hyraxes are expert climbers thanks to their unusual feet. The soles of their feet are covered in rubbery skin, which produces a lot of sticky sweat that helps the feet grip. The soles of the feet can form a sucker shape that allows the hyrax to cling onto extremely smooth surfaces.

Hyraxes usually live in rocky outcrops in the middle of scrublands. These outcrops provide good lookout points, warm spots for hyraxes to sunbathe, and lots of crevices for sleeping in or hiding from predators. Hyraxes have whiskers all over the body, so they can feel their way around in small spaces in total darkness.

Hyraxes eat all types of plant food and, like rabbits and certain hoofed animals, they have bacteria (single-celled microorganisms) in their gut. Bacteria help break down the toughest parts of plants and release the energy in the hyraxes' food.

## Living in a Group

Hyraxes live in groups and communicate using soft chattering calls and whistles. They also use scent to mark each other and their home area. For such small animals, hyraxes breed slowly. In any one year, females raise only one litter of up to three offspring. Other members of the group help by huddling close to keep the young hyraxes warm at night. Group members also keep watch for predators, such as snakes, leopards, jackals, spotted hyenas, and birds of prey.

*A hyrax has large black eyes, rounded ears, and long, touch-sensitive whiskers. If a hyrax spots danger, it produces a shrill alarm call.*

### Fact File

**HYRAXES**

**Family:** Procaviidae (11 species)

**Order:** Hyracoidea

**Where do they live?** Africa and parts of the Middle East

Equator

**Habitat:** Rocky outcrops in dry areas and forests

**Size:** Head–body length 12.5–24 inches (31–60 cm); weight 3–12 pounds (1,300–5,400 g)

**Coat:** Length and color varies with species, from short to shaggy, and from pale yellow to gray or brown; paler on the belly

**Diet:** Plants

**Breeding:** Litters of 1–3 offspring born after 7–8 months' gestation; weaned at 1–5 months; mature at 16–17 months

**Life span:** 12 years

**Status:** Three of the 11 species are listed as vulnerable

# JACKALS

Jackals are sociable, smart, and tough. Adults pair
up when young and stick together, working as a team
to find food and rear cubs. These slender, medium-sized
dogs often have a bad reputation, just as wolves do.

Jackals are related to wolves. Although slightly smaller, jackals are similar to wolves in many ways. Jackals survive well in dry habitats, where prey seems hard to find; they are not fussy eaters—they eat all sorts of different foods; and jackals are smart, agile hunters that snatch small birds and mammals and the offspring of larger animals such as antelope. Jackals also eat a lot of fruit, which provides them with water. They are great scavengers and often turn up to take a share of dead animals by roadsides. In Europe, jackals were once a common sight around graveyards, too.

## A Family Affair

Once a young adult jackal finds a mate, the pair often stays together for life, finding and then defending a territory. Jackals mark out their territory using scent and move into old, abandoned animal burrows to make dens where they can breed and rear cubs.

Both parents look after the pups, and the family moves from den to den every few days. That makes it hard for predators to find them. The pups develop fast. They are first weaned onto partly digested food, which has been coughed back up by the parents. After three months they can eat whole animals, and in six months they help their parents hunt. Young jackals leave home at around one year old, although black-backed jackals sometimes stay behind for another year to help rear the next litter and learn from their parents.

*A black-backed jackal drinks from a water hole, listening for danger. Some farmers shoot jackals because they kill lambs and other livestock.*

## Fact File

### JACKALS

*Canis aureus* (golden jackal), *Canis adjustus* (side-striped jackal), and *Canis mesomelus* (black-backed jackal)

**Family:** Canidae (3 species)

**Order:** Carnivora

**Where do they live?** Africa, the Middle East, southeastern Europe, and South Asia

Equator

**Habitat:** Grasslands, scrublands, and woodlands

**Size:** Head–body length 33–52 inches (83–132 cm); weight 14–33 pounds (6.5–15 kg)

**Coat:** Coarse, golden-fawn to gray; distinctive gray to black markings in side-striped and black-backed species

**Diet:** Small mammals, birds, reptiles, amphibians, insects, fruit, and carrion

**Breeding:** 3–4 pups born after 63 days' gestation; mature at 11 months

**Life span:** 4–8 years in the wild, and up to 16 years in zoos

**Status:** Least concern; not currently at serious risk

# JUMPING MICE, BIRCHMICE, AND JERBOAS

Some of these mice can leap 10 feet in a single bound
on their huge back feet. However, this active lifestyle
lasts for only a few months—come the fall,
they are ready to sleep for six months or more.

Jumping mice and birchmice are generally small, at no more than 4.5 inches long, but their tail is up to twice as long. They are about half the size of their cousins, the jerboas. Jumping mice and birchmice live in seasonal grasslands and forests. They spend the summer leaping around in search of food, mainly insect grubs and fungi, which they catch and eat using their front paws. The back feet of jumping mice are large and long—like those of tiny kangaroos.

## Fattening Up in the Fall

In the fall, jumping mice and birchmice fatten up on rich, oily, and sugary food, such as seeds and berries. They increase their body weight by up to one-third in just two weeks. When the food supply begins to decrease, jumping mice and birchmice hibernate in the burrow of another small mammal or find a hollow log stuffed with leaves. They sleep so deeply that they seem almost dead. Their body grows cold and their heart rate slows down to just one or two beats a minute. By using so little energy, these small animals can make their tiny store of body fat last until spring.

Jerboas live in African and Asian deserts. They breed and sleep in sand burrows, which they dig with their huge back feet. Tufts of fur on the feet act like snowshoes, helping the mice jump around on loose sand. Jerboas eat mainly seeds and fruit and get all the water they need from their food.

*A jerboa dashes across the desert. These small rodents have an extremely long, tufted tail and large hind legs for bounding along and for digging.*

## Fact File

**JUMPING MICE, BIRCHMICE, AND JERBOAS**

**Family:** Dipodidae (50 species)

**Order:** Rodentia

**Where do they live?** North America, Eastern and central Europe, northern Africa, and Asia

Equator

Jerboas—yellow
Jumping mice/
birchmice—red

**Habitat:** Meadows and other grasslands, moors, thickets, forests, and deserts

**Size:**
Head–body length 2–9  inches (5–23 cm); weight 0.2–14 ounces (6–420 g)

**Coat:** Usually coarse, but silky in jerboas; fawn to reddish or grayish brown

**Diet:** Seeds, shoots, berries, fungi, and insects and their grubs

**Breeding:** Litters of 2–6 offspring born after 17–35 days' gestation

**Life span:** Up to 2 years in jumping mice and birchmice, and 3 years in jerboas

**Status:** 7 species are at risk; some are critically endangered

# KANGAROOS AND WALLABIES

When people think of a kangaroo, they usually imagine a red kangaroo hopping across the Australian desert. But the red kangaroo is only one of seventy-six species, including many wallabies, several ratlike forest animals, and even some kangaroos that live in trees.

There are more than seventy species (types) of kangaroos. Some, such as the red kangaroo and the eastern gray kangaroo, are large and well known. But many kangaroos are small, shy, and live in remote deserts or dense forests where they are not often seen.

Kangaroos and wallabies are the most numerous and well-known marsupials. Marsupials are animals that rear their offspring in a pouch on the front of the female's body. In kangaroos, the pouch contains two teats, but usually just one baby, or joey, is born at a time. The newborn joey is tiny and furless, with undeveloped eyes, hind limbs, and tail. It crawls through its mother's fur to the pouch and latches onto a teat with its mouth. It stays there until it has grown much larger and stronger, its eyes have opened, and its fur coat has grown. It can take anything from five to eleven months for a joey to be ready to leave the pouch for good. After that, it may leave its mother to live alone or stay close by as it continues to grow.

## Kangaroo Mobs

Forest species, such as tree kangaroos and rat kangaroos, usually live alone, except for mothers with offspring. Kangaroos that live in the open in grasslands or deserts live in groups called mobs. Each group consists of one large male and several adult females and their offspring. The females are often related to each other. Young males usually leave the group when

*Always on the alert, this eastern gray kangaroo pauses while feeding to check its surroundings. It supports itself on its huge hind legs and long tail.*

### Fact File

**KANGAROOS AND WALLABIES**

**Family:** Macropodidae (76 species)

**Order:** Diprotodontia

**Where do they live?** Australia and the island of New Guinea

Equator

**Habitat:** Deserts, grasslands, scrublands, and temperate and tropical forests

**Size:** Head–body length 11–65 inches (28–165 cm); weight 1.2–200 pounds (0.5–95 kg)

**Coat:** Fine, dense, and slightly fluffy or shaggy looking; pale gray to red, brown, or black; some species have markings on the face, legs, and tail

**Diet:** Plants, including grass, leaves, shoots, seeds, roots, and fungi

**Breeding:** 1 joey (rarely twins) born after 30–39 days' gestation; reared in pouch; weaned at 4–11 months

**Life span:** Varies with species; 5–18 years in the wild, and 28 years in zoos for large species

**Status:** Gilbert's potoroo critically endangered; 9 species endangered; 12 species vulnerable

they become mature, but young female joeys stay and learn how to raise offspring from their mother and other female relatives.

### Tough Plant Food

Kangaroos and wallabies are plant eaters, but various species eat quite different sorts of plant foods. Many forest-dwelling kangaroos eat roots and tubers. Some larger species, such as gray kangaroos, euros, and pademelons, eat mainly grass. The desert-dwelling red kangaroo eats dry grass and the leaves of desert shrubs such as saltbush.

Kangaroos have bacteria (single-celled microorganisms) living in their gut that help digest tough plant material. Kangaroos spend a long time digesting their food, making sure they get as much goodness from it as possible. By making the most of every mouthful,

▷ *A red-necked wallaby joey pokes its head out of its mother's pouch. It spends many months in the safety of the pouch, coming out occasionally to hop around.*

## TWO MOUTHS TO FEED

In large kangaroos and wallabies, a joey that has left its mother's pouch still needs milk for a few more months. A joey suckles by sticking its head into the pouch to find the teat. By this time, there may be a new, younger joey in the pouch, and the two offspring use different teats. The mother kangaroo produces two different sorts of milk from each teat, so each youngster gets exactly the right nutrients.

1. Yellow-footed
   rock wallaby
2. Burrowing
   bettong, or
   boodie
3. Rufous rat
   kangaroo
4. Quokka
5. Banded hare
   wallaby
6. Proserpine
   rock wallaby

of Western Australia. These animals get all the water they need from their food or by licking up dew in the morning.

### Huge Hind Feet and Tail

Kangaroos and wallabies have small front legs and feet, with five fingers and strong claws. They use these claws for fighting, digging, and holding food. The hind legs and feet are completely different. The legs are long, with huge muscles in the thighs, which are used

they can survive on very poor food, including old dried-up grass and the tough leaves of desert shrubs. Desert kangaroos can go for weeks without drinking, as do red kangaroos and the tiny quokkas

### DID YOU KNOW?

- One-quarter of all kangaroo species live outside Australia, on the large island of New Guinea.

- Kangaroos can hop at up to 35 miles per hour!

- The group name for kangaroos and wallabies is macropod, which means "big foot" in Greek!

for hopping. The hind feet are extremely long, and each has four toes. The outer two toes are the largest, and they carry the animal's weight when it is standing or hopping. The inner two toes are fused, making a double toe with two claws. These claws are used like a comb for cleaning the fur.

As well as hopping, kangaroos can move on all fours. They lean on their front legs and swing the back ones forward. All kangaroos have a long tail. In smaller species the tail is carried off the ground and helps with the kangaroo's balance. In large species, the tail is thick and strong and can be used like an extra leg to help support the animal's weight when standing or moving around. Rock wallabies have bumpy skin on the soles of their back feet, which provides great grip, even on smooth rocks. Tree kangaroos can climb, using their front paws to grip branches and pull themselves up.

*An old kangaroo, such as this one, will have worn out and lost many of its teeth as a result of its tough plant diet.*

## KANGAROO TEETH

**Kangaroos have just one pair of front teeth, called incisors, in the lower jaw and two pairs of incisors in the upper jaw. These teeth have sharp edges and are used for cutting grass and leaves or biting chunks off roots or fruit. The cheek teeth are large and each one has a series of sharp ridges that grind food to a pulp. These teeth move forward in the kangaroo 's mouth as the animal gets older to replace worn-out teeth, which fall out.**

*A tree kangaroo snoozes in the branches of a tree.*

## Large Herbivores

Kangaroos lave a great deal in common with other large herbivores, such as antelope. Both kangaroos and antelope have grinding teeth, a long gut, and a large stomach containing bacteria to help digestion. Both also use sharp senses and speed to avoid predators. Kangaroos have eyes on the sides of the head, which give good all-round vision, and ears that turn this way and that. Kangaroos also have long legs and can move fast, making great leaps that might confuse a chasing predator. Kangaroos live alone in forests, but they live in groups in open grassland, where many pairs of eyes and ears make it hard for a predator to sneak up.

Several types of kangaroos are at risk of becoming extinct. Forest species, like tree kangaroos, have lost habitat as people clear the land for farming. Smaller species, such as potoroos, are killed by predators such as dogs and foxes brought to Australia and New Guinea by people. Red and gray kangaroos are not threatened, but sheep farmers treat them as pests. Tens of thousands are shot for meat or skins or just for sport, and many more are killed on roads every year.

# KOALA

The koala is one of the world's most loved animals, with its teddy-bear face and fluffy ears. But these cute-looking animals have a tough side, too—they are the only mammal that can survive by eating the leaves of eucalyptus trees.

Koalas spend most of the day sitting in the fork of a tree and snoozing. Some people think that koalas are lazy or even that they are affected by the poisonous chemicals present in the eucalyptus leaves they eat. The truth is that eucalyptus leaves do not contain much energy. Koalas climb slowly to save energy. The only way in which a koala can survive on eucalyptus leaves is by getting lots of rest and not rushing around. The other alternative would be to eat much more, but eucalyptus leaves take so long to digest that koalas simply do not have the time to spend eating more leaves. In addition, the leaves contain many poisonous chemicals, and it might be dangerous for a koala to eat a larger quantity of them.

## A Gripping Time

Koalas make hanging about in trees look easy. They climb by gripping the tree with all four paws, pushing up with their back legs, and pulling with their front legs. They have superb balance and can walk along narrow branches. The palms and soles of their paws are bald, and the rough skin provides excellent grip. On the front paws, the first two fingers act as thumbs, making the koala's grip strong. On the hind feet, the second and third toes are joined to make a double toe with two claws. All the fingers and toes have a large, curved, and sharp claw that hooks into tree bark. Koalas spend as little time on the ground as possible.

> *Fast asleep in the fork of a tree, this koala balances by gripping with its long, sharp claws. Koalas save energy by snoozing for most of the day and night.*

### Fact File

**KOALA**

*Phascolarctos cinereus*

**Family:** Phascolarctidae

**Order:** Diprotodontia

**Where do they live?**
Eastern Australia

Equator

**Habitat:** Eucalpytus trees

**Size:** Head–body length 23.5–33.5 inches (60–85 cm); weight 9–33 pounds (4–15 kg)

**Coat:** Fluffy and dense; usually gray with a light reddish tinge; white on chest

**Diet:** Leaves of the eucalyptus and a few other trees

**Breeding:** 1 joey born after 35 days' gestation; weaned at 6–10 months; mature at 2 years

**Life span:** Up to 18 years

**Status:** Once seriously threatened; now at lower risk

◗ *Koalas can balance on even the thinnest of branches. They spend most of their time high up in eucalyptus trees. They do not move around very much because they have a low-energy diet.*

They usually come down only to move to another tree. On the ground, they waddle on all fours, and if they have to move quickly, they break into a bouncy gallop.

Koalas live alone. Each koala uses just a few favorite trees and never wanders very far. Often, there are several unrelated koalas living in the same patch of trees. They pay very little attention to each other most of the time. That changes during the breeding season, when the largest male koala tries to drive all the other males out of his area so that he can have the females to himself for mating. Koalas are silent most of the time, but the males make loud growling calls throughout the night in the breeding season.

### Tiny Koala Joeys

After mating, a female koala is pregnant for one month before giving birth to a tiny, naked baby. A newborn koala joey weighs around the same as a single peanut. The joey

## SAVING THE KOALA

Koala fur is extremely thick and soft, and was once prized by people, who hunted the koala almost to extinction in the nineteenth century. Hunting koalas is now banned, and people are eager to protect them. The main problem now is that many of the forests where koalas live have been cut down, leaving them to survive in small, overcrowded patches where there is not enough food and where diseases spread easily.

x

*When a koala moves, it does so extremely slowly and cautiously.*

has to climb into its mother's pouch and find one of her teats. It stays there for six months, growing fast.

When the baby koala is ready to start eating solid food, its mother produces soft droppings, called pap. The baby eats the pap, which contains partly digested eucalyptus leaves. Fresh eucalyptus leaves are much too tough for the young joey to digest, and they also contain chemicals that are poisonous. By starting off on pap, the young koala's digestive system slowly gets used

to its diet. The pap also contains bacteria from the mother's gut, which stay inside the young koala and help it digest more leaves in the future.

## DID YOU KNOW?

Koalas are not bears—they are marsupials, and their closest relatives are wombats!

Koalas sometimes eat soil and gravel to help them digest their diet of leaves!

Koalas sleep for around twenty hours a day!

# GLOSSARY

**aquatic** Water living

**arboreal** Tree living

**arctic** Of, or relating to, the north pole or the surrounding region

**bacterium (plural: bacteria)** Single-celled microorganism

**baleen** Horny, curtainlike substance that hangs from the upper jaw of baleen whales; filters krill out of the seawater

**biome** Major zone of the living world, such as rain forest, desert, and temperate forest; each biome has its own distinctive climate and living organisms

**browse** To feed on the buds, shoots, leaves, and twigs of shrubs, bushes, and trees

**bull** The male of certain species, such as elephants, seals, and whales

**bush meat** The meat of wild animals hunted by local people to eat or sell

**camouflage** Pattern of coloration that allows an animal to blend in with its surroundings

**canid** Member of the family Canidae, such as coyote, dingo, fox, and wolf

**carnassial tooth** One of the two strong, pointed, slicing cheek teeth of most carnivores

**carnivore** Meat eater; animal that catches other animals for food

**carrion** Dead and decaying animal flesh eaten by other animals

**cellulose** Tough substance that makes up the cell walls of plants

**class** Major category in taxonomy ranking above order and below phylum

**classification** Organization of different organisms into related groups by biologists

**climate** Average weather conditions (temperature, wind, and rain) over a period of years

**coniferous forest** Area of cone-bearing trees that grow mainly in cold regions of the northern hemisphere

**crustacean** Water-living creature (for example, crab, water flea, and shrimp)

**cud** Food brought up from the stomach for a second chewing, usually by plant eaters such as cows and sheep

**desert** Major biome, or type of ecological community, covering around one-seventh of Earth's surface; has few plants and less than 10 inches of rainfall each year; hot or cold region that is extremely dry

**dew claw** Extra digit ("finger" or "toe")

**digestion** The breakdown of food into small, easily absorbed molecules in the digestive system

**DNA** Deoxyribonucleic acid; present in the cell nuclei of a living organism; carries inherited genes

**domesticated** Farmed

**dominant** Highest-ranking

**dormant** Being in a state of suspended biological activity

**echolocation** Use of sound echoes to build a picture of the surroundings by animals such as bats and dolphins

**ectotherm** Cold-blooded animal; *see also* endotherm

**embryo** Early stage of a mammal while it is inside the mother's womb

**endangered species** Any species that is extremely close to becoming extinct in the wild

**endotherm** Warm-blooded animal; *see also* ectotherm

**equator** An imaginary line around the widest part of Earth that is equally distant from the north and south poles and which divides the surface equally into the northern and southern hemispheres

**estivation** An animal's sleeplike resting state in summer to avoid heat and drought; *see also* hibernation

**Eurasia** Europe and Asia

**evolution** The way in which species of living organisms change over long periods of time

**extinct** Any species that has not been found in the wild for an extremely long time and which is therefore thought to have disappeared forever
**extinction** Death of a species of living organism

**family** Group of related living organisms forming a category ranking above a genus and below an order
**feces** Expelled waste products of digestion
**feral** Wild animal descended from a domesticated animal that returned to the wild
**fossil** Evidence of past life preserved in tar, peat, amber, rock, or volcanic ash

**gene** Section of DNA that codes for one inherited characteristic
**genus** Group of closely related species
**gestation** The time an animal spends developing inside its mother (pregnancy)

**habitat** Type of place in which an animal or plant usually lives or grows
**herbivore** Plant-eating animal
**hibernation** To spend the winter in an inactive, or dormant, sleeplike state; *see also* estivation
**home range** Area usually covered by an individual animal during a particular period of its life; *see also* range

**insectivore** Insect-eating mammal, such as an aardvark or anteater
**invertebrate** Animal without a backbone

**joey** Young kangaroo or wallaby

**krill** Shrimplike, planktonic animal life that floats in the oceans and forms the main food of baleen whales

**litter** Multiple offspring of a single pregnancy

**mammary gland** Milk-producing gland present in the skin of mammals
**metabolism** The chemical changes in living cells that provide energy for essential life processes such as growth and repair
**migration** Seasonal, long-distance journey by animals, such as wildebeests and whales, often to feed or breed
**molt** Shed (as in coat)

**New World** Geographical term referring to the western hemisphere, particularly North, Central, and South America; *see also* Old World
**niche** A lifestyle particular to a specific species
**nocturnal** Active at night
**northern hemisphere** Half of Earth north of the equator
**nutrient** Food vital for an animal's chemical life processes

**Old World** Geographical term referring to the eastern hemisphere, comprising Europe, Africa, and Asia; *see also* New World
**omnivore** Mammal that eats both plants and animals
**order** Category of taxonomic classification ranking above family and below class

**phylum** Category of taxonomic classification ranking above class and below kingdom
**placenta** Temporary organ that develops in the womb to allow a mammalian embryo to obtain nourishment from the mother during gestation
**plankton** Microscopic animal and plantlike life in the ocean
**pollination** Transfer of pollen from the male to the female parts of a flower
**predator** Animal that kills and eats other animals
**prehensile** Grasping (as in digit or tail)
**prey** Animal caught and eaten by another animal

**primate** Member of the mammalian order Primates; includes apes, bush babies (galagos), humans, lemurs, lorises, monkeys, pottos, and tarsiers

**rain forest** Major biome, mostly in the tropics; high annual rainfall; tall, fast-growing trees that form an overhead canopy; daytime temperature is usually 90°F; annual rainfall is greater than 70 inches

**range** Geographic area within which members of a species usually live; *see also* home range

**rodent** Member of the order Rodentia, including agoutis, beavers, capybaras, guinea pigs, hamsters, mice, rats, squirrels, and voles

**rumen** Large first compartment of a ruminant's stomach, which contains microorganisms that break down cellulose

**ruminant** Mammal that chews the cud; for example, camels, cows, and sheep

**saliva** Watery mouth secretion

**savanna** Tropical grassland biome with scattered trees and shrubs in Africa, South America, and Australia

**sediment** Material deposited by water, wind, or glaciers

**shrubland** Biome containing plants such as short trees and shrubs

**southern hemisphere** Half of Earth south of the equator

**species** Scientific term meaning a kind or type of organism that can breed to produce offspring that can also interbreed successfully

**steppe** Extensive temperate grassland biome present in Europe and Asia

**subspecies** Local type

**taiga** Major biome present in northern Canada, southern Alaska, Scandinavia, Siberia, and parts of Japan; mostly evergreen forests, bogs, marshes, and small lakes

**teat** Nipple of a mammary gland

**temperate grassland** Large area within temperate zone covered with grass

**temperate rain forest** Woodland area within temperate zone covered with dense growth of trees and brush, with heavy annual rainfall

**temperate zone** Region between the Tropic of Cancer and the arctic circle or between the Tropic of Capricorn and the antarctic circle

**territory** Area occupied by a single animal or group of animals of the same species

**threatened species** Any species that is at risk of becoming endangered

**tropical forest** Woodlands of tall, broadleaved, evergreen trees forming a continuous canopy that receive at least 100 inches of rain each year; includes rain forests; present in the Amazon region of South America, parts of Africa (Democratic Republic of the Congo, Congo, Gabon, Cameroon), and Asia (Indonesia, Papua New Guinea, and Myanmar)

**tropical grassland** Savanna, which lies north and south of equatorial tropical rain forests

**tundra** Major treeless biome characterized by dark soil with a permanently frozen subsoil and plants such as lichens, mosses, herbs, and dwarf shrubs; present across the northern coasts of Alaska, Canada, Greenland, Scandinavia, and Russia

**vertebrate** Animal with a backbone

**wean** To change from a diet of mother's milk to alternative, more solid food; begin eating solid food

**womb** Organ in female mammals in which unborn mammals develop (uterus)

# FURTHER RESOURCES

## BOOKS

Beer, Amy-Jane and Pat Morris. *Encyclopedia of North American Mammals.* San Diego: Thunder Bay Press, 2004.

Dutcher, Jim, J. Dutcher, et al. *Living with Wolves.* Seattle, Washington: Mountaineers Books, 2005.

Evans, P. J. H. *Marine Mammals: Biology and Conservation.* New York: Plenum Press, 2001.

Forsyth, Adrian. *Mammals of North America: Temperate and Arctic Regions.* Ontario, Canada: Firefly Books, 2006.

Fossey, Dian. *Gorillas in the Mist* (new ed.). London: Phoenix/Orion, 2001.

Goodall, Jane. *In the Shadow of Man* (new edition). London: Phoenix/Orion, 1999.

Graham, Gary. *Bats of the World (Golden Guide).* New York: St. Martin's Press, 2001.

Greensmith, Alan, and J. Clutton-Brock. *Mammals.* Dorling Kindersley, 2002.

Kingdon, Jonathan. *The Kingdon Pocket Guide to African Mammals.* Princeton Pocket Guides. Princeton, NJ: Princeton University Press, 2005.

Reid, Fiona. *Peterson Field Guide to Mammals of North America* (4th ed.). Boston: Houghton Mifflin, 2006.

Rosing, Norbert. *The World of the Polar Bear.* London: Christopher Helm/A & C Black, 2006.

Scott, Jonathan, and A. Scott. *Big Cat Diary: Cheetah.* London: Collins/BBC, 2006.

Turner, A. *National Geographic Prehistoric Mammals.* Washington: National Geographic Children's Books, 2004.

## INTERNET RESOURCES

**All About Mammals**
Check out mammals, their evolution, and classification.
www.enchantedlearning.com/subjects/mammals

**American Museum of Natural History**
Visit the mammal halls and travel across continents.
www.amnh.org/exhibitions/permanent/mammals/

**Animal Diversity Web**
A general site with sections on mammals; search facility for species.
animaldiversity.ummz.umich.edu/site/index.html

**Australian Museum Online**
Find out about Australia's marsupial mammals.
www.amonline.net.au/mammals

**BatAtlas**
Information about bats.
online.anu.edu.au/srmes/wildlife/batatlas.html

**BBC Science and Nature: Animals**
Features a mammals site based on the television series by David Attenborough.
www.bbc.co.uk/nature/animals/mammals

**BigCats.Com**
Online guide to wild cats.
bigcats.com

**Canid Specialist Group**
Information on wild dogs.
www.canids.org

**Cetacea**
Online guide to dolphins, porpoises, and whales; includes a guide to whale watching.
www.cetacea.org

**Dian Fossey Gorilla Fund International**
Conservation of gorillas and their habitats.
www.gorillafund.org/index.php

**Elephants of Africa**
Information, contests, and puzzles on the life of elephants.
www.pbs.org/wnet/nature/elephants

**eNature Field Guides**
The U.S. National Wildlife Federation Web site features mammals of North America.
www.enature.com/home

**Fossil Horses in Cyberspace**
Virtual museum exhibit examining the evolution of horses.
www.flmnh.ufl.edu/natsci/vertpaleo/fhc/fhc.htm

**IUCN Red List of Threatened Species**
Worldwide assessment of the conservation status of species of living organisms.
www.iucnredlist.org

**National Primate Research Center, University of Wisconsin**
Find out about primates.
pin.primate.wisc.edu/aboutp

**National Wildlife Federation**
Gray wolves in North America.
www.nawa.org/about_wolves.html

**Seal Conservation Society**
Conservation news about seals.
www.pinnipeds.org

**Smithsonian Institution National Museum of Natural History**
A searchable database of all living mammals of North America.
www.mnh.si.edu/mna

**Tasmanian mammals**
Details on bats, whales, monotremes, marsupials, and rodents living in Tasmania.
www.dpiw.tas.gov.au/inter.nsf/ThemeNodes/LBUN-5362ZN?open

**Ultimate Ungulate Page**
Find out about the world's hoofed mammals, including hyraxes, elephants, dugongs, and many others.
www.ultimateungulate.com

**World Wildlife Fund**
Find out more about wildlife conservation.
www.worldwildlife.org

# INDEX